GIVING
THE DEVIL
HIS DUE

GIVING THE DEVIL HIS DUE

Demonic Authority
in the Fiction of Flannery O'Connor
and Fyodor Dostoevsky

JESSICA HOOTEN WILSON

 CASCADE *Books* · Eugene, Oregon

GIVING THE DEVIL HIS DUE
Demonic Authority in the Fiction of Flannery O'Connor and Fyodor Dostoevsky

Cascade Books
An Imprint of Wipf and Stock Publishers
199 W. 8th Ave., Suite 3
Eugene, OR 97401

www.wipfandstock.com

PAPERBACK ISBN: 978-1-4982-9137-8
HARDCOVER ISBN: 978-1-4982-9139-2
EBOOK ISBN: 978-1-4982-9138-5

Cataloguing-in-Publication data:

Names: Wilson, Jessica Hooten.

Title: Giving the devil his due : demonic authority in the fiction of Flannery O'Connor and Fyodor Dostoevsky / Jessica Hooten Wilson.

Description: Eugene, OR: Cascade Books, 2017 | Includes bibliographical references and index.

Identifiers: ISBN 978-1-4982-9137-8 (paperback) | ISBN 978-1-4982-9139-2 (hardcover) | ISBN 978-1-4982-9138-5 (ebook)

Subjects: LCSH: 1. Criticism, interpretation, etc. | 2. Fyodor Dostoevsky, 1821–1881. | 3. Flannery O'Connor, 1925–1964. | I. Title.

Classification: PR99 W26 2017 (paperback) | CALL NUMBER (ebook)

Manufactured in the U.S.A.   02/24/17

Parts of chapter three were originally published as "Demonic Authority of the Autonomous Self in O'Connor and Dostoevsky" in *Flannery O'Connor Review* 8 (2010) 117–129.

For my parents, Rick and Evelyn Hooten

Not unto us, O LORD, not unto us, but unto thy name give glory, for thy mercy, and for thy truth's sake.

—Psalm 115:1 (King James Version)

Contents

Acknowledgements

THIS BOOK IS PREDICATED on the idea of mimesis, that we all have models whom we imitate either volitionally or not. I am grateful for the many people who have modelled a love for the true, good, and beautiful in my life, who have shown me how not only to study these things but also to live by them. Many of my ideas are not my own but a compilation of teachers and writers whose voices are in dialogue within me. I would like to acknowledge as many of them as I can for their direct influence on this particular idea and their help in bringing this manuscript to publication.

My introduction to Fyodor Dostoevsky came in 2004 in a Russian literature seminar at Pepperdine University, where I was an undergraduate. Paul Contino led my class through *The Brothers Karamazov* (along with Tolstoy's *War and Peace*), and I became hooked on the Russians. Flannery O'Connor, on the other hand, has been a longtime love since I was fifteen years old.

The idea for this book began forming in 2005 when I attended Louise Cowan's Russian literature course, as well as her course on Southern writers at the University of Dallas. Cowan was a masterful teacher and intellectual who dug beneath the surface of texts to find the deep-down true things. She was the first to show me—unintentionally—the connections between Dostoevsky and O'Connor. Two years later, when I began my dissertation on these authors, she invited me to spend an hour with her discussing these masters. The conversation was rich, personal, and beneficial in ways that I cannot quantify. I will be forever grateful for her generosity towards me.

This book began as a dissertation, and I want to thank my committee from Baylor University for all of their feedback and guidance: Luke Ferretter, Sarah Ford, Peter Chandler, David Lyle Jeffrey (who pointed me towards Rene Girard!), and Ralph Wood, my director. Ralph deserves more thanks than I can muster in a brief paragraph. Working closely with Ralph on this project transformed it from a long, rambling paper into a sensible, worthwhile book. His commentary was brutally honest. He persevered with me despite my shortcomings initially as an author, and he compelled me towards excellence. Without him, this book would not exist.

I would like to also acknowledge the many colleagues who responded with their encouragement and critiques throughout the process, including but surely not limited to Sarah-Jane Murray, Susan Srigley, and Margy Thomas Horton, each of whom helped me find my academic voice. In 2009 I presented part of Chapter One at the Poetics and Christianity Conference in Rome, Italy, after which Hank Edmondson helped shape the ideas into their current form. At the same conference, the comments of Bill Sessions were heartening, especially his personal tales of O'Connor's admiration of Dostoevsky and his suggestion that I look to her unpublished novel *Why do the Heathen Rage?*, which Bill considers her most Dostoevskian work.

In spring 2016, I received the help of Annaleta Nichols, who worked meticulously to copy edit, check citations, and format the manuscript for publication. I hope she considers her hard work to have paid off; I'm grateful for her efforts.

Finally, I should conclude this list of gratitude with thanks to my parents for believing in my project, even when the idea of putting a Russian and Southern writer together sounded like nonsense to most everybody else, to my husband Jonathon for not begrudging me the evening, weekend, and holiday hours to work on the scholarship I love, and to my children for their patience as I tapped away at a computer screen before reading Dr. Seuss "just one more time."

INTRODUCTION

AT THE MERE MENTION of Flannery O'Connor and Fyodor Dostoevsky, some people experience distaste, revulsion, or horror. People accuse the writers of being dark, violent, and even misanthropic. As a scholar of these two authors, I often hear remarks such as, "Ick, O'Connor—all those dead bodies," or, "You smile too much to be a Dostoevsky scholar." On the other hand, the readers who love these two authors often deem them to be saints, elevate their works to the status of near-biblical revelation, make pilgrimages to their grave sites, and display memorabilia on office walls and computer screens. Both O'Connor and Dostoevsky may have expected their audiences' aversion, but they would have been ill at ease with the adulation. After all, they set out to expose the comfortable lies that had been digested by their generations and to replace these lies with ancient truths from Christian Scripture. Those who attempt to imitate Christ should expect the world to hate them for it.[1]

Although from different sects of the church, both were passionately devoted Christians: O'Connor was a cradle-born Roman Catholic, and Dostoevsky was Russian Orthodox, and became more devout following a conversion in prison. While the rest of the world was becoming progressively secular, these two remained loyal to their faiths and considered their art to be their vocation. Neither succumbed to the popular accommodation of church doctrine, as will be shown later—although Dostoevsky was swayed for a brief period of his life by Christian Socialism, only to turn 180 degrees from it. And, it is the faith of these two writers that undergirds not only their aesthetic visions but also their themes and ideas. The way in which these two writers set about putting their faith into fiction has been discussed *ad nauseum* by many scholars, but I want to look more closely

---

1. 1 John 3:13, NIV, "Do not be surprised if the world hates you."

at how their faith led them to unveil a modern deception—that of the autonomous self.

To elucidate their common revelations, I turn to the work of René Girard, who first discovered the lie of the autonomous self when reading Dostoevsky. Originally a French literary scholar, Girard branched into cultural criticism in 1961 when he published his first book *Deceit, Desire and the Novel*, an examination of five novelists, including Dostoevsky. Girard uncovered the nature of conversion in the novelists' work.[2] Following his investigation of the novels of Dostoevsky in particular, Girard underwent a conversion himself not only of intellect but also of spirit. In Girard's assessment, the novelists converted from the lie of absolute autonomy to the truth that all human beings are essentially mimetic creatures who imitate the desires of others. The French title of this first book *Mensonge romantique et verite romanesque* translates to "romantic lie and novelistic truth," key themes in his theory on mimetic desire.[3] For Girard, the "romantic lie" bought and sold by most modern novelists is that of the autonomous self whereas the "novelistic truth" unveiled by great literature is the opposite, the mimetic nature of each human being.

In *René Girard and Secular Modernity*, Scott Cowdell gives a brief but accurate description of "secular modernity" in the Western world that shows how religion's hold on society disintegrated from the late Middle Ages until now. His accounts attempt to pull together the narratives put forward by thinkers such as Richard Dawkins and, on the other end of the spectrum, by Charles Taylor. While versions of the story emphasize alternately the developments in science, or changes in economic structures, or moves in government towards democratization, most seem to recognize secularization as the increase in personal autonomy accompanied by a variety of alternative metanarratives from the Judeo-Christian one. This world in which God is not the authority for society, nor the Alpha and Omega for individual persons, is labeled "secular." However, Cowdell offers a caveat via Girard. In Girard's theory, the greater autonomy of the modern self is an illusion. "Girard sees secular modernity in the West as functionally

2. Wolfgang Palaver summarizes Girard's argument for "an existential connection between the great works of literature and the lives of the authors that created them" in his book *René Girard's Mimetic Theory*, 2.

3. Scott Cowdell indicates this literal translation in his book *René Girard and Secular Modernity*, 171.

religious," Cowdell notes, though its religion is based on a sovereign self versus a divine authority.[4]

Girard's theory has developed and evolved since 1961 and been extended into numerous other arenas of the academy (which this book will not delve into). For my purposes, I will look at his discoveries as they pertain to literature, mostly to those found in Dostoevsky that may be extracted and applied to O'Connor. As previously stated, in summary, Girard asserts that all human beings imitate the desires of others, whether or not they acknowledge the imitation. Behind his theory are theological assumptions based on Judeo-Christian Scriptures.[5] Girard clarifies these suppositions in a handful of his works, including *The Scapegoat, I See Satan Fall Like Lightning,* and *Things Hidden Since the Beginning of the World.* Rather than quote extensively from numerous sources, I will delineate his assertions here. According to Girard, because God created humans in his image, a model exists from the beginning that we can embrace or deny. In biblical accounts, one of God's angels, Lucifer, denied the authority of God, denied being a creature and considered himself an autonomous individual. Satan, as he became known, established himself as an alternative model. When the Son of God renounced his high place in the Trinity to appear historically on earth as Jesus Christ, he countered this model—not with a showcase of power but with humility by becoming a victim to the violence of those who followed Satan. Thus, the choice of whether to follow Christ or Satan is also whether to be humble or proud, whether to be truthful or blind, and whether to suffer or cause violence.

The same choice that Girard is convinced lies before human beings, whether to imitate Christ or Satan, underlies all of O'Connor's and Dostoevsky's respective works. In Dostoevsky, his character Ivan Karamazov famously reduces the choice when he says, "Without God, all is permissible." One watches as the notorious Ivan, who has accepted his own premise, is driven mad by the devil on his shoulder. In O'Connor, The Misfit in "A Good Man is Hard to Find" echoes the choice with Girardian language: "If [Jesus] did what He said then its nothing for you to do but . . . *follow him,* and if He didn't then its nothing for you to do but enjoy the few minutes

4. Ibid., 12.

5. "From the beginning, Girard's position is rooted in biblical thinking" (Palaver, *René Girard's Mimetic Theory,* 28). I will not be dealing with Girard's biblical commentary. Palaver does a good job summarizing his work on the Old and New Testament.

you got left the best you can—by *killing somebody*."[6] Such a choice sits uncomfortably with the readers of O'Connor and Dostoevsky who want to inhabit a middle ground.

O'Connor and Dostoevsky scandalize the modern reader by portraying this unwanted truth to readers. The either/or choice outlined by Girard and presented by these authors does not allow for the possibility that someone could be a good person without following Jesus Christ, or could be an autonomous individual who also believes in Jesus as God.[7] Readers question whether the choice is so limited. However, Girard asserts, "If we don't see that the choice is inevitable between two supreme models, God and the devil, then we have already chosen the devil and his mimetic violence."[8] When Ivan decries the terms of God's harmony and returns his ticket, he becomes not only possessed by a devil but also complicit in his father's murder. In O'Connor's novels, Hazel Motes denounces Jesus as a liar to found the Church without Christ, and then he justifies the homicide of Solace Layfield with his own moral system. Similarly, in O'Connor's second novel, after Rayber asserts that religion is insubstantial propaganda used to control and restrain a person's natural and good intuitions, he finds himself unable to validate his son Bishop's existence and later becomes complicit in filicide. In Dostoevsky and O'Connor's fiction, the Christian life is not one option among many; rather, it is the only alternative to violence.

The truth that Girard discovers in Dostoevsky is the same truth that O'Connor propagates in her fiction. Few critics have examined her work in this light. In 2007 Susan Srigley relied on Girard to take readers beneath the surface of O'Connor's scandalous fiction to understand the source of violence and the possibility of self-sacrifice as a way to bear it.[9] Gary Ciuba also used a Girardian lens to view the violence of a host of modern Southern authors, including Walker Percy and Cormac McCarthy, as well as O'Connor in her second novel *The Violent Bear It Away*.[10] Most recently, Jeremiah Alberg concluded his book that uses Girard's theory as a way to read authors as varied as Plato, Dante, Rousseau, and the New Testament

6. O'Connor, *Collected Works*, 151.

7. Palaver points out that Girard's first book is prefaced in the French original with a phrase by Max Scheler: "Man believes in either a God or in an idol. There is no third course open!" (*René Girard's Mimetic Theory*, 27). This either/or without a third option is embodied in Dostoevsky's and O'Connor's fiction.

8. Girard, *I See Satan Fall Like Lightning*, 24.

9. Srigley, "The Violence of Love."

10. Ciuba, *Desire, Violence, & Divinity in Modern Southern Fiction*.

authors, with an examination of O'Connor.[11] With Girard's theoretical paradigm, these scholars have been able to overcome the scandal of O'Connor's fiction and illuminate the truth in her stories. Rather than stumble over mutilated corpses and encounters with a litany of freaks, as many readers do, I would like to join these critics in applying Girard's theory to shine light on seemingly dark stories, and perhaps to alter paradigms for readers who, as O'Connor would say, have "hold of the wrong horror."[12]

In addition to the numerous connections between Dostoevsky and O'Connor, the fact that Girard made his discoveries from reading Dostoevsky makes a joint consideration of the authors even more compelling. However, if one were to weigh Dostoevsky's output beside O'Connor's, it would be an unfair scale. Not only did Dostoevsky live twenty years longer (1821–1881) than did O'Connor (1925–1964), but also he specialized in novels whereas her primary genre was the short story. His extended lifespan and lengthy genre choice means that, quantitatively, he exceeded her literary output. Therefore, of all of Dostoevsky's oeuvre, I will focus on his final novel *The Brothers Karamazov*, which Girard and others have regarded as "the masterwork of its author."[13] In this last book, Dostoevsky achieves all that he intended with his previous novels. Whereas his earlier fiction shares similar themes with *The Brothers Karamazov*, all comes to fruition in this final masterpiece.

CONNECTIONS BETWEEN DOSTOEVSKY'S AND O'CONNOR'S WORLDS

While I derive much of my comparison from the authors' theological visions, their cultures also have important parallels. As unlikely as it may first sound, nineteenth-century Russia shares a surprising amount in common with the twentieth-century South. In 1941 Southern author Carson McCullers asserted, "The circumstances under which Southern literature has been produced are strikingly like those under which Russians functioned."[14] Through an evaluation of a scene from Dostoevsky's *Crime and Punishment* with that of Faulkner's *As I Lay Dying*, McCullers shows how alike Russian and Southern fiction are as well as the cultures that produced them. Mc-

---

11. Alberg, *Beneath the Veil*.

12. O'Connor, *The Habit of Being*, 90.

13. Girard, *Resurrection from the Underground*, 56.

14. McCullers, "The Russian Realists and Southern Literature," 252.

Cullers explains that both societies are dominated by a "cheapness of human life," though she does not elaborate much more on this feature. In a presentation on nineteenth-century Russian literature and modern Southern writers, Bertram Wyatt-Brown suggests that this cheapness of human life stems from the hierarchical social order apparent in Russian feudality and the Southern practice of slavery. He notes, "Such a social order produced a feeling of utter indifference to cruelty and even to the humanity of lesser members of society."[15] In 1861 Russia abolished serfdom, and two years later America followed suit, the largest changes occurring in the American South (it should be noted that Russia and America are two of the last world powers to abolish slavery). These abrupt and violent revolutions in the class system transpired simultaneously with the Russian military disasters of the Crimean episode that parallel the Southern defeat in the American Civil War. Wyatt-Brown notes that these conflicts "exposed the weakness of the czarist empire, which had long prided itself, like the slave states of America, on its military prowess."[16] The changes accompanying the defeats of both regions produced similar cultural environments.

Because of their losses, both Russia and the South lacked the progressive and future-looking attitudes of their counterparts, Europe and the North respectively. Whereas nineteenth-century Europeans and twentieth-century Northerners acknowledged no limits their potential accomplishments, their counterparts were less optimistic. They knew that pride often preceded a fall. In O'Connor's essay "The Regional Writer" she explains what she believes her fellow Southerner Walker Percy meant in his 1961 National Book Award acceptance speech:

> When Walker Percy won the National Book Award, newsmen asked him why there were so many good Southern writers and he said, "Because we lost the War." He didn't mean simply that a lost war makes good subject matter. What he was saying was that we have had our Fall.[17]

For the post-Civil War South, they saw their way of life come burning down, literally, as Sherman set plantation homes ablaze. The fall exemplified their descent from the "cotton is king" world to dependence on the North for economic reconstruction. In his study of Russia's cultural influence, Steven

15. Wyatt-Brown, "Nineteenth-Century Russian Literature and Modern Southern Writers," 201–14. Personal copy.

16. Ibid., 4.

17. O'Connor, *Mystery and Manners*, 59.

G. Marks explains the affect of the South's "fall": "From [Southern writers'] vantage point in a South still agonizing over its loss in the Civil War, they had imbibed an assumption of fallen man and original sin, which gave them a darker view of the world than that reflected in much of American fiction."[18] By contrast, Northern writers believed that the American dream was an attainable future, exemplified in works like *The Great Gatsby* with the "orgastic future" that could be reached "tomorrow [when] we will run faster, stretch out arms farther."[19] Southerners did not identify with the novels of the culture that lay only a few miles across the Mason-Dixon as much as with the one that existed oceans and generations away. Instead, the novels of Dostoevsky provided a countercultural model that resonated with many Southern writers.[20]

During the Southern Renascence, Southern authors from Faulkner to Percy emulated Dostoevsky. On the strength of Dostoevsky's influence in the South, Wyatt-Brown writes, "[Dostoevsky] loomed so large that Southern writers experienced what Harold Bloom identified many years ago as the anxiety of influence."[21] From the Russian perspective, A. N. Nikoliukin concurs, "[A]fter the First World War, Dostoevsky suddenly proved alone the most influential writer in America."[22] When Carson McCullers assesses the Russian influence on Southern literature, she focuses on Dostoevsky. In her mind, the grotesque, or what she terms "Gothic," style of his work that most attracted Southerners. She analyzes the juxtaposition of the tragic and absurd in the scene from *Crime and Punishment* where Marmeladov's mourners eat dinner together, comparing it to Faulkner's *As I Lay Dying*, where Anse Burden and his children are more concerned about false teeth, dessert cake, and gangrene than about their deceased mother lying in the back of the wagon. She refers to both writers' realism as "bold and outwardly callous juxtaposition of the tragic with the humourous, the immense with the trivial, the sacred with the bawdy, the whole soul of a man

18. Marks, *How Russia Shaped the Modern World*, 92.

19. Fitzgerald, *The Great Gatsby*, 191–92.

20. "Dostoevsky's example showed Southern writers, if they required any more convincing, that they need not conform to Northern or European models or expectations, but could set their own literary norms." (Bloshteyn, *The Making of a Counter-Cultural Icon*, 6.)

21. Wyatt-Brown, "Nineteenth Century Russian Literature and Modern Southern Writers," 17.

22. Nikoliukin, *Vzaimosviazi literature Rossii I SShA* [*Interrelations of Russian and American Literatures*], 239.

with a materialistic detail."[23] Considering this realism an inheritance from the Russians, particularly Dostoevsky, McCullers proposes it is rare except in Russian and Southern literature.

O'CONNOR'S READING OF DOSTOEVSKY

O'Connor first read Dostoevsky in graduate school at the University of Iowa in 1945 as an exemplary novelist for emulation.[24] At the time, he was being popularly disseminated by Modern Library as a "new" author because translations of his work into English had only recently been released.[25] In addition to Dostoevsky's posthumous literary success among American readers, at that time, producers from Hollywood to Broadway were transferring his work to screen and stage.[26] Among the literary elite, Dostoevsky was being read with fervor. Bloshteyn has documented his influence on Henry Miller, the Beat poets, African American writers such as Ralph Ellison, and Southerners en masse.[27] In 1955, the topic was interesting enough for *The New York Times* reporter Harvey Breit to inquire about it in a televised interview with O'Connor. When Breit asks whether O'Connor thinks there's something to the connection between her contemporary South and the Russia of the nineteenth century, she responds tersely, "I think there is."[28]

23. McCullers, "The Russian Realists," 253.

24. O'Connor lists Dostoevsky among the many canonical authors to whom she was introduced in graduate school (*The Habit of Being*, 98–99). She also owned a copy of Joseph Warren Beach's *Twentieth-Century Novel* in which Dostoevsky is studied as a precursor to modern fiction. O'Connor may have read this in her Iowa Workshop. She has underlined page 98 on Dostoevsky, in which Beach writes, "We draw this conclusion without the least prompting by the author." In her own fiction, O'Connor seems to employ this lesson of avoiding prescribed interpretations for readers.

25. On January 31, 1938, *TIME* magazine cited the publisher Bennet Cerf's assertion that "Dostoevsky's *The Brothers Karamazov* is the most popular of the Modern Library's 257 titles, [and] has sold 120,000 copies in ten years."

26. For example, in 1958 MGM released *The Brothers Karamazov* starring Yul Brynner.

27. Bloshteyn has published *The Making of Counter-Cultural Icon: Henry Miller's Dostoevsky*, 277–309; and "Dostoevsky and the Literature of the American South," 1–24.

28. The conversation is recorded in Rosemary Magee's collection *Conversations with O'Connor* (8) as well as in a video recording held in the O'Connor collection at Georgia College and State University.

Although O'Connor never claims that Dostoevsky influenced her writing, she does cite him throughout her letters as a favorite author.[29] Her laconic response in the interview with Breit is in keeping with her comments concerning her other influences. She tended to confess only the subliminal impact of authors on her, for example Henry James and Joseph Conrad, who would "affect [her] writing without [her] being bothered knowing how."[30] This jest concerning Conrad contains additional irony, since Conrad, despite his protest to the contrary, is often likened to Dostoevsky. O'Connor admits two other influences that also have been tied to Dostoevsky: Edgar Allan Poe and Nikolai Gogol.[31] At O'Connor's death, three of Dostoevsky's books were in her personal library, *Crime and Punishment*, *The Possessed*, and *The Best Short Stories of Dostoevsky*, though we know, because of her letters and essays, that she also read *The Brothers Karamazov* and *The Idiot*. (Regrettably, she never annotated these texts or reviewed any of Dostoevsky's work.) Whether O'Connor consciously imitated Dostoevsky is not the question here because this is not an influence study; however, what is crucial here is that O'Connor did absorb his work, could reference him without a book in hand, and understood him better than her Southern counterparts who mostly saw him merely as a grotesque author.

29. In a 1960 interview with Robert Donner, he writes of O'Connor: "Among her favorite authors are Dostoievsky and Hawthorne, and she returns to them at regular intervals" (Magee, 47). In a letter to Ted Spivey (Nov. 16, 1958), she references *The Brothers Karamazov*: "But in the Legend, Dostoevsky is using the Inquisition as a figure for the whole Church" (*The Habit of Being*, 304). First, when O'Connor bought *The Idiot*, she records a conversation with her mother (Feb. 1, 1953), and in a letter to Father J. H. McCown (Aug. 5, 1962), she alludes to a character: "She says Msgr. [Illych] is straight out of Dostoevsky" (*The Habit of Being*, 488). Finally, even with little time to read, she chooses to reread Dostoevsky (Apr. 27, 1963): "It seems to me I don't have much time to read. I intend to read Dostoevsky this summer ..." (*The Habit of Being*, 515).

30. O'Connor, *The Habit of Being*, 63.

31. In discussing her literary influences, O'Connor mentions Edgar Allan Poe: "always the largest thing that looms up is *The Humerous Tales of Edgar Allan Poe* [sic]" (*The Habit of Being*, 98). In a 1962 interview, O'Connor says, "I'm sure Gogol influenced me" (Magee, *Conversations*, 94). Dostoevsky also read much of Poe, as Madina Tlostanova writes in "The Russian 'Fate' of Southern Letters, or Southern Fiction and 'Soviet' Diction": "Poe, who began to be translated and published in Russia in the 1840s, was truly 'discovered' first by Dostoevsky" (28). Belinsky writes that Dostoevsky "as a writer of great talent cannot be called an imitator of Gogol though he certainly owes a great deal to him" (quoted in Magarshack's introduction to *Dostoevsky's Short Stories*, xiv).

The multitudinous similarities between Dostoevsky's and O'Connor's grotesque would fill a separate volume. O'Connor showcases her debt to Dostoevsky in the combination of such disparate elements, the comic and terrible, which she describes as "opposite sides of the same coin."[32] She explains (September 24, 1955), "In my own experience, everything funny I have written is more terrible than it is funny, or only funny because it is terrible, or only terrible because it is funny."[33] Steiner makes a similar claim about Dostoevsky's fiction, using the word "fantastic" rather than "comic": "In Dostoevsky's novels, we cannot separate 'the tragic' from 'the fantastic.'"[34] Other Southern authors, such as McCullers, reproduce this feature but without the same intention as Dostoevsky, a motivation that O'Connor shares.

The few pieces written on the style of O'Connor and Dostoevsky miss the purpose behind their styles. In her master's thesis on O'Connor and Dostoevsky,[35] Katherine Hemple Prown discusses three shared literary techniques: their use of doubles, such as Ivan and Smerdyakov and Tarwater and Rayber, their ironic humor, and the epiphanic scenes.[36] In a brief essay on Dostoevsky and Southern women writers, Temira Pachmuss lists more similarities, noting that like Dostoevsky, O'Connor employs:

> hallucinations and dreams, often mysterious and incomprehensible, and has recurrent types of characters and situations in her novels and short stories. Her art is religiously oriented, and death plays an important role in it as a strong spiritual experience,

---

32. O'Connor, *Collected Works,* 957.

33. Ibid.

34. Steiner, *Tolstoy or Dostoevsky,* 211.

35. Prown, *Flannery O'Connor, Fyodor Dostoevsky, and the Anti-Modernist Tradition.* In roughly forty pages, Prown does not have enough space to elaborate on all her various conclusions, and her study is limited by a negative thesis, for Prown defines O'Connor and Dostoevsky in terms of what they are against rather than what they are for. While O'Connor and Dostoevsky illustrate the weaknesses of the modern world, neither writer is necessarily antimodernist. Both reject the modern form of atheism though not modernism itself. Stylistically, Dostoevsky may be called a progenitor of modernism and O'Connor a descendent.

36. Norman McMillan also analyzes these aspects in an article on O'Connor's "Revelation." ("Dostoevskian Vision in Flannery O'Connor's 'Revelation.'") McMillan lists fifteen critics in his footnote who have also "noted in passing an affinity between the two authors," although none "of these critics argues that O'Connor was directly influenced by Dostoevsky, but all seem to assume a shared vision" (16).

imparting clarity to the visions that torment her characters during their lifetimes.[37]

Yet, these similarities continue. These scholars neglect to mention that O'Connor and Dostoevsky both create deformed characters—prostitutes, idiots, holy fools, and social pariahs—to explore such problems as the suffering of children as a refutation to God's existence, the moral bankruptcy of modern atheism, the universal parricidal impulse, the demonic as a real force, and the potential for grace to manifest itself in the natural realm. Moreover, O'Connor's and Dostoevsky's fiction is steeped in biblical language and imagery; both writers refer to Christ dozens of times in their texts and introduce morally ambiguous Christ figures. Their characters engage in serious philosophical discussions that border on the absurd, searching for and often denying a transcendent order. What is most important to this study is the common purpose of Dostoevsky's and O'Connor's aesthetic.

DOSTOEVSKY'S AND O'CONNOR'S INCARNATIONAL AESTHETIC

In the early part of the twentieth century, Dostoevsky's literary style was largely ignored, sometimes tolerated, but definitely not considered worthy of imitation. In the original Russian, Dostoevsky uses countless gerunds and participles, packing sentences full of phrases and clauses like a traveler stuffing suitcases to the point that shirttails stick out of the corners. Russian translator Constance Garnett toned down his aspects of his style in order to popularize him. Her friend John Galsworthy expresses to Edward Garnett how uncomfortable the original Russian is:

> I'm rereading *The Brothers Karamazov* a second time; and just after *War and Peace*, I'm bound to say it doesn't wash. Amazing in places, but my God!—what incoherence and what verbiage, and what starting of monsters out of holes to make you shudder.[38]

Galsworthy's comments on *The Brothers Karamazov* resemble those of Allen Tate after reading O'Connor's *Wise Blood*. Tate says in his 1964 tribute to O'Connor, "I hadn't the vaguest idea of what she was up to; I offered to

---

37. Pachmuss, "Dostoevsky and America's Southern Women Writers," 120. Like Prown's thesis, Pachmuss's article focuses on O'Connor's and Dostoevsky's depictions of the absurdity of the godless world.

38. Quoted in May, *The Translator in the Text*, 33.

correct her grammar; I even told her that her style was dull, the sentences being flat and simple declarative. No doubt what I said was true; but it was irrelevant."[39] Tate points beyond O'Connor's style to her *vision*. Both Garnett and Tate understood the meaning in Dostoevsky's and O'Connor's work, respectively, but these critics did not understand how the authors' literary styles acted as conduits for their ideas.

Whatever their critics may have assumed, Dostoevsky and O'Connor did attend to their aesthetics of their craft. They considered themselves to be realists, albeit not in the same sense that literary theorists often use the term. Dostoevsky describes himself as a "realist in the higher sense," and O'Connor calls herself a "realist of distances." Neither refuted their use of the grotesque, but they tried to explain the purpose for their readers. In his notebooks, Dostoevsky clarifies, "I am only a realist in the higher sense; that is, I portray all the depths of the human soul."[40] Dostoevsky's higher realism correlates with O'Connor's realism of distances. She writes:

> In the novelist's case, prophecy is a matter of seeing near things with their extension of meaning and thus of seeing far things close up. The prophet is a realist of distances, and it is this kind of realism that you find in the best modern instances of the grotesque.[41]

O'Connor's realism, like Dostoevsky's, brings meaning to the surface; it makes the meaning inseparable from the narrative. Their versions of realism are what some writers have called incarnational or sacramental art.[42]

Dostoevsky's and O'Connor's realism can be said to have an incarnational character for three reasons: the motivation on the part of the artist to imitate God, not only as Creator but also as Christ in humility to his or her vocation; the higher realism of the work itself that depicts the everyday world as invested with spiritual significance; and the hope for conversion within the observer or reader that he or she may receive changed vision from the revelation imparted by the artist. Girard's theory of mimesis is helpful here. First, if artists recognize their mimetic nature, then they volitionally imitate the real world in their fictional creations. Christian artists

---

39. Back, *The Fugitive Legacy*, 233.

40. Quoted in Simmons, *Introduction to Russian Realism*, 104.

41. O'Connor, *Collected Works*, 817.

42. Christina Bieber Lake has written *The Incarnational Art of Flannery O'Connor*, and Susan Srigley has written *Flannery O'Connor's Sacramental Art*. Also, Paul Contino uses the phrase "Incarnational Realism" to discuss Dostoevsky's *The Brothers Karamazov* in "Incarnational Realism and the Case for Casuistry," 131–58.

do so with the theological underpinning that this imitation is of the God who created this world in the beginning. On the other hand, artists may deceive themselves that they are creators ex nihilo, without prior influences and designers of wholly new creations. This is the romantic fallacy. Such distortion leads an artist to create idolatry, which leads readers to fantasy or false ideology. Of course, the possibility for reader misinterpretation always exists in spite of the author's intention. Alberg notes, "All great authors are keenly aware of the potential for evil in literature," and he lists examples that Girard has discussed, such as Francesca and Paolo from Dante's *Inferno* who blame the story of Lancelot and Guinevere as the cause for their adultery.[43] Because the readers are mimetic creatures as well, authors should be cautious of what vision of the world that they present. In considering Dostoevsky's and O'Connor's aesthetic, then, the work must be discussed with all three facets considered—the author's desire, the text itself, and the reader's response.

Of Dostoevsky's desire to believe in Christ, we have no doubt, although some critics, including Girard, debate the authenticity of Dostoevsky's faith. Girard concludes that even though Dostoevsky "badly wanted to be a real Christian, genuine religious faith kept eluding him."[44] Girard writes this conclusion despite all of Dostoevsky's declarations to the contrary. In an 1854 letter, following his release from Siberian prison, Dostoevsky famously asserted, "If someone proved to me that Christ is outside the truth, and that *in reality* the truth were outside of Christ, then I would prefer to remain with Christ than with the truth."[45] Twenty years later, he reclaims his faith in Christ in his notebook, illustrating the continuity of his belief: "[I]t is not like a child that I believe in Christ and profess faith in him, but my *hosanna* has come through a great *crucible of doubt*."[46] In letters and in his *Diary of a Writer*, Dostoevsky publicly abhorred the misuse of Christian Scripture and asserted his belief in Christ. Moreover, he read and marked his New Testament often, as can be seen in his personal editions of the Bible, and he made regular pilgrimages to monasteries.[47]

43. Alberg, *Beneath the Veil*, 109.

44. Girard, *Resurrection*, 87.

45. Quoted by Joseph Frank, *Dostoevsky: A Writer in His Time*, 913.

46. Ibid.

47. There are numerous sources on Dostoevsky's religion, though it is best to start with Joseph Frank's biography to see the full picture. The best collection of essays on Dostoevsky is by editors George Pattison and Diane Oenning Thompson, *Dostoevsky and the Christian Tradition*. The discussion of Dostoevsky's Bible markings is in an article

Similarly, O'Connor professes her faith not only in her letters, interviews, and essays but also by her regular attendance at mass, daily prayers, and participation in church sacraments.[48] When she visited Lourdes in 1958, she prayed more for her second novel than she did for her failing bones: "I would rather finish this novel right than be able to walk at all."[49] However, like Dostoevsky's "crucible of doubt," O'Connor admits to uncertainty. She writes, "I can only say with Peter, 'Lord I believe, help my unbelief.'"[50] In 1962 John Hawkes challenged readings of O'Connor as a pious author, insinuating that, as Milton was in *Paradise Lost*, she too was of the devil's party without knowing it.[51] O'Connor refuted Hawkes, but following this article, a slew of critics leapt into dispute whether or not O'Connor was as Christian of an author as she professed. Whether or not her work showcases faith as readers believe it ought to, biographically, she is viewed as an orthodox Christian.

Disputes over the faiths of both Dostoevsky and O'Connor ensue because these authors can and do showcase the "other side"; they give the demonic a fair hearing, and make evil appear powerfully real. Nothing frustrates first-time readers of O'Connor and Dostoevsky as much as the convincing portrayals of the demonic. Like Hawkes asserting that O'Connor is of the devil's party, writers such as D. H. Lawrence protest that Dostoevsky's Grand Inquisitor is the victorious voice in *The Brothers Karamazov*.[52] Attuned to the invisible world and surrendering to a realism that stems from it, both writers depict the universe as a choice between good and evil. For both Dostoevsky and O'Connor, their commitment to imitating Christ means depicting the truth with all its scandal, with all of its opportunity for doubt. In the Gospels, Christ himself seems to profess doubt on the cross when he calls out to God, "Why have you forsaken me?"[53] Because the fiction writer's role is to represent life as it is, this picture must include as much dark as light.

---

found there by Irina Kirillova, 41–50.

48. Jonathan Rogers has paid particular attention to O'Connor's faith in his spiritual biography of her, *The Terrible Speed of Mercy*.

49. O'Connor, *The Habit of Being*, 310.

50. Ibid., 92.

51. Hawkes, "Flannery O'Connor's Devil," 395–407.

52. Lawrence, "Preface to Dostoevsky's *The Grand Inquisitor*," 233–46.

53. Matt 27:46 (NIV).

In addition to confusing the novice reader, O'Connor and Dostoevsky's illustrations of dark and light compel seasoned scholars and theologians to interpret their work as Manichean. Girard disputes this rendering, in the case of Dostoevsky, using terms that should apply equally to O'Connor: "To say that [their work] reveals good and evil as pure choice is to say that no Manicheanism remains in it. We feel that at any moment Ivan might save himself and Alyosha could be lost"[54]—so, too may Tarwater cremate his uncle or Rayber yell out in dismay over the murder of his son. The characters in these works may clash, but their unfinalizability keeps them from becoming reduced caricatures of good and evil. In his famous study of Dostoevsky, Mikhail Bakhtin discusses these features more fully.[55]

O'Connor herself informs readers how to view the "moments of grace" in which she extends choice to seemingly damned or self-condemned characters.[56] In her analysis of "A Good Man is Hard to Find," O'Connor interprets the grandmother's final gesture to be such an acceptance of grace. The counterpart in the story is The Misfit, the serial killer, who may or may not be changed by his dialogue with the grandmother, but grace is offered as much to him as it is to her. While O'Connor and Dostoevsky portray both good and evil within their works, there is no clear line between heroes and villains. As Alberg rightly points out in his book on Girard, "Any interpretation in which we know who the good guys and who the bad guys are weakens the story's import."[57] Rather than a simplistic morality tale, the aesthetic realism of Dostoevsky and O'Connor compels these authors to offer the choice between good and evil to all characters, and thus vicariously to readers.

The choice is whether to see clearly, which would be to submit to a world in which the character is not the autonomous authority but rather the creature made in the image of a higher God. Such a vision of the world often reflects an accompanying and unwanted image of the self as prideful and imperfect, which we will return to later. These two competing visions of the world are aligned with that of Christ or of the devil. In his discussion of Dostoevsky's Inquisitor, Girard writes, "The pinnacle of diabolic lucidity is also extreme blindness."[58] Those who believe they have the clearest

---

54. Girard, *Resurrection*, 71.

55. Bakhtin, *Problems of Dostoevsky's Poetics*.

56. O'Connor, *Mystery and Manners*, 112.

57. Alberg, *Beneath the Veil*, 89.

58. Girard, *Resurrection*, 69.

vision, like the Pharisees who accost Christ in the Gospels, are often the most blind.[59] And, like the Pharisees who strictly followed the Lord's commandments, even those who contend to be faithful believers are susceptible to blindness.[60] For Girard, this vision is demonic because the person falling prey to such blindness has chosen to imitate Satan, the depriver of vision, the great deceiver and father of lies: "If we don't see that the choice is inevitable between the two supreme models, then we have already chosen the devil."[61] O'Connor acknowledges that her audience are those who suffer such blindness, which dictates her role as a writer "to draw very large, simple caricatures" in the hope that the same moment of grace may occur for the reader as for the character.[62]

Analogously, the choice for whether to submit to God as authority and imitate Christ transpires in the life of the artist. Girard sees the protagonist as manifesting the trajectory of the author: "The final conversion of the hero is a transposition of the novelist's fundamental experience, of his renunciation of his own idols, of his own spiritual metamorphosis."[63] While writing the novel, the author has been constantly confronted with choices for how to imitate the created order as well as how, as an artist, to be humble or to project oneself upon the text. Girard finds evidence, in literature produced since the Renaissance, of this Promethean assertion of creative will, of the poet's illusion that he alone creates from his individual essence. In contrast to this Romantic paradigm, Girard exalts Dostoevsky as the writer who undergoes a "new conversion" with each novel that he writes, being constantly transformed by the "spiritual experience" of writing.[64] According to Dostoevsky's and O'Connor's comments on their own work, art should be a discovery of truth. They believe that the revelations delivered to their characters are those they themselves received. O'Connor

59. In the Gospel of John 9:41 (NIV), Jesus tells the Pharisees: "If you were blind, you would not be guilty of sin, but now that you claim you can see, your guilt remains." The pride that compels them to claim perfect sight reveals their blindness.

60. Girard, *I See Satan*, 42: "Many people believe they are faithful to Jesus, and yet they address superficial reproaches to the Gospels. This shows that they remain subject to mimetic rivalries and their violent one-upmanship." Girard's assertion here likens modern believers to the Pharisees in their "superficial" understanding of the New Testament and what it means for their lives.

61. Ibid.

62. O'Connor, *Mystery and Manners*, 34.

63. Girard, *To Double Business Bound*, 4.

64. O'Connor, *Resurrection*, 4, 72.

insists on the truth to be found in stories: "Stories don't lie when left to themselves. Everything has to be subordinated to a whole which is not you. Any story I reveal myself completely in will be a bad story."[65] Within this one letter, O'Connor exhibits her desire for truth, her submission to something greater than herself, and her distaste for Romantic self-expression.

In addition to the intentions of the authors, the works themselves illustrate the incarnational aesthetic in their organization, style, and theme. In Girard's notes on Dostoevsky's final novel, he writes, "[T]he structure of *The Brothers Karamazov* is close to the form of *The Confessions* and *The Divine Comedy*. It is the structure of the *incarnation*."[66] Girard indicates that all of these works follow the movement of descent preceding ascent: like Christ who moved from his position in heaven to be lowered to earth, suffer death, and then rise again to rejoin the father, so Augustine falls into sin only to be transformed by the Gospels into a Christian convert and eventual bishop, and so Dante descends into hell first on his journey that then culminates in paradise. So, too, in Dostoevsky's work, all three Karamazov brothers embody the epigraph from John 12:24: "Unless a grain of wheat falls to the ground and dies, it remains only a single seed. But if it dies, it bears much fruit."[67] The paradoxical nature of the incarnation expressed by these writers is that descent, usually through suffering and death, precedes ascent.

In O'Connor's world, the descent is as literal as it is spiritual. Her characters fall down, often into pits, before being lifted into light. Richard Giannone[68] lists the numerous pits in O'Connor's stories and connects them with Dante's inferno, but not without also tying them to the ascent up Mount Purgatory: "In effect, O'Connor's ditch combines the geography of Dante's descending hell with the psychology of his rising Mount Purgatory." For instance, Hazel Motes is found in a ditch preceding Mrs. Flood's deep stare into his eyes, where she finds the infinite light. The grandmother in "A Good Man is Hard to Find" stumbles into a ditch before she reaches up to The Misfit as one of her own children. In O'Connor, the incarnational aesthetic affects the literal movement of her characters as well as their spiritual moves.

---

65. O'Connor, *The Habit of Being*, 105.

66. Girard, *Resurrection*, 72, emphasis mine.

67 Paul Contino makes this argument in "'Descend that You May Ascend,'" 179–214.

68. Giannone, "Dark Night, Dark Faith."

Also O'Connor exhibits her incarnational realism in the mingling of the dirty particulars with the sublime and transcendent. As I mentioned before, the ditch becomes the setting for revelation. Elsewhere it is Mrs. Turpin washing of her pigs that fosters a vision of the afterlife or a tattoo parlor as the site for Parker's encounter with Christ. Erich Auerbach's book *Mimesis* analyzes the mimetic realism in the Old and New Testaments, which is reflected in the styles of Dostoevsky and O'Connor. O'Connor read his book (Feb. 11, 1958), recommending to Sally and Robert Fitzgerald the "chapter on the style of the *Odyssey* contrasted with the style of the Old Testament."[69] In this chapter, Auerbach suggests that the Old Testament is more realistic than Homer's epic because the writers bring the meaning to the foreground. He writes, "The sublime influence of God here [in the Old Testament] reaches so deeply in to the everyday that the two realms of the sublime and the everyday are not only actually unseparated but basically inseparable."[70] God is not merely a character in these stories; his presence affects the plot, the actions of other characters, and the meaning behind these actions.

When Auerbach discusses the New Testament, he describes how its authors increase the unification of the sublime and prosaic. He calls this unification a "mingling of styles," which was

> rooted from the beginning in the character of Jewish-Christian literature; it was graphically and harshly dramatized through God's incarnation in a human being of the humblest stations, through his existence on earth amid humble everyday people and conditions, through his passion which, judged by earthly standards, was ignominious; and it naturally came to have . . . a most decisive bearing upon man's conception of the tragic and the sublime.[71]

The incarnation of Jesus Christ defines the style of the New Testament narratives. Although the stories occur in the dirtiness of the real world, they claim spiritual and universal importance. Moreover, the story of Christ's incarnation inverts traditional notions of the tragic and the sublime. In his discussion of the Russian writers, Auerbach concludes that Dostoevsky is

---

69. O'Connor, *The Habit of Being,* 267. O'Connor probably recommended this chapter because Robert Fitzgerald was working on his translation of *The Odyssey*, which he published in 1961.

70. Auerbach, *Mimesis,* 23.

71. Ibid., 41.

more of a Christian than an occidental realist.[72] As with the New Testament authors, for Dostoevsky and O'Connor, the incarnation compels them to write in the grotesque or higher realist style.

The most scandalous aspect of Dostoevsky's and O'Connor's incarnational realism is the prioritization of the unseen reality over the empirically known world. If readers attempt to excise the transcendent from the worlds that these authors create, their interpretations of the texts will appear inconsistent and their authors insane. In an interpretation that misses the reality of Dostoevsky's story, for instance, Sigmund Freud writes Dostoevsky off as a latent homosexual who has a problematic relationship with his father.[73] The devil's visit to Ivan must be only hallucination, psychological disorder, or madness if there is no such thing as a demon. To read Zosima, moreover, one would have to dispense with all of his good deeds and sayings as delusions, for his entire belief system would be seen as merely a comforting mythos. Most challenging of all, for readers without a belief in another world, is Dostoevsky's depictions of death. When Illyusha dies, the arguments of Ivan are not triumphant. Instead of tallying him alongside Ivan's list of suffering children, Alyosha exalts him as one who has gained an immortal victory. Dostoevsky reconfigures death, so that the conclusion of the novel is not tragic but comic. Yet, Dostoevsky leaves the choice with his readers between seeing as Ivan does, and thus being aligned with the demonically possessed, or seeing through the eyes of Alyosha.

In O'Connor, the problem intensifies, as she felt her audience was more hostile and unbelieving than that of Dostoevsky. While she may not have desired for her work to scandalize readers, she knew the difficulty twentieth-century readers would face in confronting the truth. In her Author's Note for the second edition of *Wise Blood*, O'Connor writes, "That belief in Christ is to some a matter of life and death has been a stumbling block[74] for readers who would prefer to think it a matter of no great consequence." The stumbling block occurs because O'Connor, like Dostoevsky before her, forces her readers to consider questions of belief. In his Girardian reading of O'Connor, Alberg uplifts these "stumbling blocks of offense" as "bridges

---

72. Ibid., 521: "Russian realism . . . is fundamentally related rather to Old-Christian than to modern occidental realism."

73. Freud, "Dostoevsky and Parricide," 104.

74. One of Girard's theories is that the biblical word "scandal," translated as "stumbling block," should be understood as Satan's contrivance to cause humans to fall.

into the deeper meaning of the mystery of Christ."[75] When violence shocks readers in O'Connor's stories, she hopes they will not stay shocked, that instead the shock will bring them into deeper understanding. If Mrs. May is gored by a bull for no reason, then the story is an object of horror. However, if readers consider the transcendent reality that O'Connor portrays, then the suffering and violence become less important than the grace revealed.[76]

Although O'Connor claims to write for those who believe that God is dead,[77] she also asserts elsewhere that her audience shares her familiarity with Scripture. Initially those two statements may appear contradictory, but when understood together, they indict the contemporary Christian culture as much as nineteenth-century philosopher Frederick Nietzsche's original Madman did. The Madman, in "The Gay Science," initially seeks God and finds him nowhere. He then calls out, "*We have killed [God]*—you and I. All of us are his murderers,*" condemning everyone of deicide.[78] When the crowds remain silent upon hearing this news, the Madman concludes that he has come too soon. In this same piece, the Madman calls the churches the tombs of God. For Nietzsche, who Girard labels "the most anti-Christian philosopher," it is not the atheists who have removed God from his temple, but it is the Christians.[79] Unfortunately, the audience who ignored Nietzsche's Madman still holds their spots in the pews. In *Bad Religion*, New York Times columnist Ross Douthat points out that America, in particular, is not overrun by those without religion, but by those with *bad religion*, with the heretical belief that they are in charge of their own religion. The murder of God was a subtle strangling in which the "Christian" slowly assumed more and more of the demonic belief in his or her autonomy.

In the twentieth century, the "death of God" occurred quietly in pulpits while violent deaths outnumbered all preceding counts of violence in every other century. To many, the two facts are unconnected. Moreover, these same blind viewers see the pride of the individual as no longer a vice but a virtue, and one that is unrelated to either the death of God or to the systemic violence of our culture. Since the autonomy of the individual is an accepted

75. Alberg, *Beneath the Veil*, 91: Alberg is speaking about the Gospels in this section, but he later applies this way of reading to O'Connor's fiction.

76. Alberg (ibid.) posits that readers are scandalized by O'Connor's juxtaposition of violence and grace: "confronted with her violent overcoming of scandal, [readers] can see only the violence and not what is being overcome," 101.

77. O'Connor, *The Habit of Being*, 92.

78. Nietzsche, *The Portable Nietzsche*, 96.

79. Girard, *I See Satan*, 163.

illusion, woe to the novelist who reflects the image of Satan as its source. For all of the aforementioned reasons, Dostoevsky's and O'Connor's fiction is scandalous, but not least of all, because of the violence and possession of which they accuse their readers. However, Dostoevsky and O'Connor illustrate that the death of God is a false victory for the autonomous self because this autonomy is actually slavery to a demonic contagion, to use Girard's terms. By reading Dostoevsky alongside O'Connor, we can unravel how this dethroning of God and increase in violence occurs and perhaps map a way back to love and mercy.

CHAPTER OUTLINE

In the first chapter, I examine Dostoevsky's Ivan Karamazov and O'Connor's Rayber, who justify their rejection of God's authority with a protest on behalf of those who suffer. Although both Dostoevsky and O'Connor admit the strength of these characters' argument, they reveal that when this sympathy for the suffering is founded on a source outside of Christ, it will unwittingly lead to further suffering. Because these characters cannot see themselves in the victim and refuse to imitate the only God who understands suffering, they instead try to play God in their plans for world improvement. Ivan's Inquisitor is a mere starting point for the Russian Revolution, and Rayber's theories could easily be mistaken for Nazi rhetoric. In *I See Satan Fall Like Lightning*, Girard ties the same arguments made by Ivan and Rayber with that of Nietzsche and the Nazis, showing not only that the concern for victims cannot be founded outside of Christianity but also how such concern is linked, ironically, to the horrors of the Holocaust.

In chapter two, I address the violence in Dostoevsky's and O'Connor's work. Girard maintains that human beings will act as wolves towards one another when God is not the mimetic model, and Dostoevsky's *The Brothers Karamazov* and O'Connor's fiction offer the best portrayal of this truth. In Dostoevsky's novel, the denial of God culminates in the parricide of Fyodor Karamazov. O'Connor extends this prophecy further in *Wise Blood* in which Hazel Motes founds a Church without Christ. A Girardian reading of the novel reveals the extent to which violence stems from mimetic rivalry, as well as the problems with autonomous individualism, and the possibility of bearing away that violence. Also in this chapter, O'Connor's short stories will be briefly examined for their illustration of how this individualism is prevalent in the modern world and how it undermines God's established order.

Most controversially, in chapter three, I will reveal that Dostoevsky and O'Connor show this autonomy to be not only violent but also demonic. Although talk of Satan and devils is usually reserved for fundamentalist extremists, Dostoevsky and O'Connor both take the demonic seriously in their fiction. Girard's understanding of Satan as the generator mimetic rivalry, lies, and destruction clarifies how the demonic works in these two authors' stories. In *The Violent Bear It Away*, the devil presents Tarwater with the choice between the two authorities: "It ain't Jesus or the devil. It's Jesus or *you*."[80] His statement is, of course, like everything the devil says, both true and false. When one establishes herself against Jesus, she has been subsumed by the devil. In both this second novel and in Dostoevsky's final novel, the devil appears and so challenges the modern assumption about his nonexistence.

In conclusion, Dostoevsky and O'Connor offer an alternative to imitating Satan—the imitation of Christ. According to Girard, modeling Christ is the means of relinquishing satanic pride. Because Jesus Christ desires to model God the Father, he "invites us to imitate his own imitation," as Girard phrases it: "What Jesus invites us to imitate is his own *desire*, the spirit that directs him toward the goal on which his intention is fixed: to resemble God the Father as much as possible."[81] As the Son of God, Jesus offers the perfect model for submitting to the Father. In my conclusion, I will emphasize those characters in O'Connor and Dostoevsky who submit their wills to the will of God. Just as Job moves from condemning God for his suffering to submitting his own finite judgment to the infinite wisdom of God, so too these characters relinquish their selfish pride for a life of love.

80. O'Connor, *Collected Works*, 354.
81. Girard, *I See Satan*, 13.

CHAPTER 1

Using Suffering to Protest God's Authority

Flannery O'Connor privileges her 1961 introduction to *A Memoir of Mary Ann* as possessing secrets for unlocking her fiction: "In the future, anybody who writes anything about me is going to have to read everything that I have written in order to make legitimate criticism, even and particularly the Mary Ann piece."[1] The memoir is a collection of anecdotes by Dominican nuns that recounts the short life of Mary Ann, a child with terminal cancer. While O'Connor's claim may seem too large for such a small piece, in this introduction, she establishes the crux of her thoughts on suffering and the mercy of God. The scandal of her piece lies in her contention that those most vehement against violence may be the very perpetuators of it. In the only direct allusion to Dostoevsky in her published work, O'Connor marks Ivan Karamazov as the rebel who, on the basis of human justice, dethrones God:

> One of the tendencies of our age is to use the suffering of children to discredit the goodness of God, and once you have discredited His goodness, you are done with Him. . . . Ivan Karamazov cannot believe, as long as one child is in torment. . . . In the absence of this faith now, we govern by tenderness. It is a tenderness which, long since cut off from the person of Christ, is wrapped in theory. When tenderness is detached from the source of tenderness, its

1. O'Connor, *The Habit of Being*, 442.

23

logical outcome is terror. It ends in forced labor camps and in the fumes of the gas chamber.[2]

In this brief paragraph, O'Connor denounces the foundation of Ivan's protest, his love for suffering children, as theoretical and insubstantial. She uses him as a prototype of those who rationalize away God's existence, and thus leave us without a source for genuine love. In God's absence, we create our own versions of love, what Dostoevsky's Father Zosima calls "love in dreams" and what O'Connor labels tenderness "wrapped in theory." Establishing himself by default as the paragon of goodness, Ivan unwittingly opens the door to further immorality. This paragraph is packed with complicated ideas about O'Connor's theodicy, which she attempts to unveil in the character of Rayber, her own version of Ivan Karamazov, in her second novel *The Violent Bear It Away*. By comparing the two characters, we can trace how O'Connor may draw a line from Ivan's atheistic dissent from God to the horrors of the Holocaust.

While Dostoevsky may not be conflated with his character, Ivan does present the argument that Dostoevsky believed was the greatest against God's goodness. "My hero chooses a theme *I* consider irrefutable: the senselessness of children's suffering," Dostoevsky writes. However, they differ in that Ivan "develops from it the absurdity of all historical reality."[3] In contrast to Ivan, Dostoevsky hoped to show how to live as a Christian in the face of suffering.[4] Yet, his motivation was not drawn from some abstract place apart from the reality of pain and sadness but from experiencing it himself. In 1878, shortly before Dostoevsky began to write *The Brothers Karamazov*, his three-year-old son Alyosha died in an epileptic fit. Following the funeral, Dostoevsky retreated to Optina Pustyn monastery. This was the second child that Dostoevsky had lost, but this death caused him greater suffering than he had previously known.[5] His wife Anna Grigoryevna writes, "My husband was crushed by this death. He had loved Alyosha somehow in a special way, with an almost morbid love. . . . What

2. O'Connor, *Mystery and Manners*, 226–27.

3. A letter to N. A. Lyubimov, No. 660, Staraya Russa, May 10, 1879. Cited in Matlaw's edition of *The Brothers Karamazov*, 757–58.

4. In a letter to his editors (June 11, 1879), Dostoevsky persuades them that Ivan's rebellion will not win out. He hopes Zosima's deathbed scene will show "that Christianity is the only refuge of the Russian land and its evils. I pray God I'll succeed. The whole novel is being written for its sake." Quoted by Frank in *Dostoevsky: A Writer in His Time*, 792.

5. Ibid. Dostoevsky tells his brother: "I am sadder than I have ever been."

racked him particularly was the fact that the child had died of epilepsy—a disease inherited from him."[6] Weighted by sorrow and emotional guilt over his child's death, Dostoevsky commenced writing *The Brothers Karamazov*. Rather than composing a novel that glosses over suffering or presents an easy answer to the problem, Dostoevsky lends the stage to Ivan and allows him to dispute God's goodness.

Likewise, O'Connor could have used her suffering to object to the design of God's world. Diagnosed with lupus at age twenty-five, O'Connor returned to her mother's home in Georgia to spend the next fourteen years on crutches and constantly in the hospital or undergoing surgery. As the disease began to set in, she quips (March 17, 1953), "I can with one eye squinted take it all as a blessing."[7] But, near the end of her life, she laments (May 28, 1964), "I am sick of being sick."[8] Although she must strain to see the good, O'Connor does not reject God's goodness. She came to affirm her ironic blessing, as she writes (June 28, 1956): "Sickness before death is a very appropriate thing and I think those who don't have it miss one of God's mercies."[9] O'Connor does not sugarcoat the suffering that she went through, nor does she sanitize the problem of violence in her work. In her fiction, she confronts difficult passages from the Bible, such as Herod's slaying of hundreds of newborns, and recent examples of violence that are completely irrational, such as Auschwitz. With an "unsentimental eye of acceptance," she still chooses faith in Christ.[10]

PROTEST ON BEHALF OF THE SUFFERING INNOCENT

Ivan Karamazov is famous for his rebellion against God. In *The Brothers Karamazov*, Ivan is a sulky man in his early twenties who has said very little, though much has been said about him. His ideas, which will be further explicated later on, have caused quite a stir among the intelligentsia. The narrator calls him a "genius" who has a notable "unusual and brilliant aptitude for learning"[11] and exhibits "practical and intellectual superiority

---

6. Frank, *Dostoevsky: The Mantle of the Prophet*, 383.

7. O'Connor, *The Habit of Being*, 57.

8. Ibid., 581.

9. Ibid., 163.

10. O'Connor, *Collected Works*, 830–31.

11. Dostoevsky, *The Brothers Karamazov*, 15.

over that eternally needy and miserable mass of our students."[12] The irony in this tone hints at Ivan's perception of his intellectual gifts, perhaps to a fault. From his youth, Ivan receives high marks in school, and, at university, he publishes articles in journals. He gains a reputation for his learning, esteeming himself for his intellectual accomplishments as much as the outside world does.

In her second novel, O'Connor creates a "latter-day Ivan Karamazov"[13] in the schoolteacher George Rayber, who also prides himself in his intellect. Rayber has attended graduate school, and like Ivan, has published his thoughts for public consumption.[14] His uncle Old Mason Tarwater is a backwoods prophet who says that "every living thing that passed through [Rayber's] eyes into his head was turned by his brain into a book or a paper or a chart."[15] Under the guise of charity, Old Tarwater once resided with Rayber, only to be turned into a case study for Rayber's publication. Rayber's primary objective in the novel is to save his nephew, Francis Marion Tarwater, the bastard and orphaned child of Rayber's sister, from the influence of Old Tarwater. His determination to "raise [young Tarwater] according to his own ideas"[16] parallels Ivan's refusal to surrender Alyosha to Father Zosima's authority.

Although Alyosha is the audience for Ivan's dissent, Ivan establishes his debate against Father Zosima and the Christian "side" of the argument. Ivan states his intentions plainly, "I won't give you up to your Zosima."[17] What begins as a confession morphs into a rant in which Ivan tries to justify his point of view to his brother in the hopes that he may persuade him to his perspective and away from the Christian worldview embodied by Alyosha's beloved elder Father Zosima. In opposition to what Ivan assumes is Zosima's position, Ivan wants to seduce Alyosha both emotionally and intellectually into seeing God as unjust and viewing suffering as an incomprehensible and unavoidable impasse.

Rather than a dialogue, Ivan seems to be holding a lecture on the correctness of his views of God and the world. Rayber does not even pretend

12. Ibid., 16.

13. Wood, *Flannery O'Connor and the Christ-Haunted South*, 195.

14. O'Connor, *Collected Works*, 392.

15. Ibid., 341.

16. Ibid., 331.

17. Ivan states, "I simply wanted to put you in my perspective" (*The Brothers Karamazov*, 237).

to discuss the issue with young Tarwater. Because Rayber shares Ivan's self-assurance and certainty about the wrongness of Christian teachings, he fortifies himself against the other side, and closes himself off to any discussion with his uncle, Old Mason Tarwater, who describes Rayber's mind as a "penitentiary" set against him.[18] Ivan's adamant stance in opposition to Christianity recalls the words of John Ames, the elderly preacher from Marilyn Robinson's *Gilead*. As the old man is accosted by a self-proclaimed agnostic and reputed prodigal son, Ames observes, "[N]othing true can be said about God from a posture of defense."[19] In the case of Ivan, his observation is correct for Ivan seems deaf to any points outside of his own perspective. Rayber, who is literally deaf in one ear, symbolizes this closed-mindedness when he switches off his hearing aid rather than listen to the "Word of God" being preached.[20]

Like a fallacious rhetorician asserting a majority of unnamed supporters, Ivan assumes a "numberless multitude of other people" agree with him.[21] For the sake of brevity, he limits his argument to the suffering of children for they are innocent, whereas, it could be reasoned that adults suffer because of their own evil deeds, or as Ivan phrases it, they have "become 'as gods,'" a reference to the fall of Adam and Eve in Genesis 3:5, as well as an allusion to the demonic serpent's temptation for knowledge of "good and evil."[22] In opposition to adults "who have eaten the apple," the innocent children should not suffer for their parents' transgressions. Ivan adamantly exclaims, "It is impossible that a blameless one should suffer for another, and such a blameless one!"[23] When Dostoevsky interprets this scene in letters, he reminds readers that Ivan is young. His passion has, in the author's words, "strained his heart to the utmost so as not to break forth."[24] Like a college student who has recently discovered social injustice,

---

18. O'Connor, *Collected Works*, 374. In one of his recollections about Rayber, Old Tarwater notes that, at twenty-four, Rayber was still open to the gospel. In *The Brothers Karamazov*, Ivan is twenty-four. His youth opens up more possibility for change in his character than Rayber's age does.

19. Robinson, *Gilead*, 202.

20. O'Connor, *Collected Works*, 415: When Lucette Carmody is preaching, Rayber snaps "the switch that would cut off the voice."

21. Dostoevsky, *The Brothers Karamazov*, 237.

22. Ibid.

23. Ibid., 238: When Ivan uses the word "impossible," he means it "must not" happen. Russians use the phrase idiomatically in this sense.

24. Dostoevsky, *The Diary of A Writer*, 791.

Ivan feels the suffering of these innocents, ironically, exhibiting the empathy that he fears is impossible. Perhaps thinking of his own suffering under his buffoon of a father, Fyodor, Ivan relates to these children, and he rages against a world in which the father's sins are borne by the children.

Few have noticed that Ivan's objection stems from his own suffering. The narrator notes that he speaks in a "delirium," and Ivan excuses his remarks as being caused by his headache and unexplained sadness.[25] Hesitant to admit his own needs, Ivan poses a hypothetical situation to Alyosha at the start of their conversation: "I, for example, am capable of profound suffering, but another man will never be able to know the degree of my suffering because he is another and not me."[26] Ivan regards suffering as an alienating experience one must undergo alone. He cannot imagine empathy as a reality or the sharing of one another's burdens, for he interprets even acts of charity as "self-laceration" and not self-giving or selfless love.[27] Despite his intellectual assertions, however, Ivan offers another possibility for why he undertakes this dialogue with Alyosha: "perhaps I want to be healed by you."[28] This desire alludes to the sickness that Ivan suffers from, an emotional depression that is later revealed as demonic possession. When Ivan admits this option to Alyosha, he smiles "like a meek little boy,"[29] a description that connects him to the suffering children on whose behalf he cries out. In these two sentences, the narrator reveals that Ivan too is a suffering child, who longs for an answer to his questions as well as a cure for what ails him. Although Ivan reaches out to Alyosha for help, he ultimately believes that his suffering isolates him from others.

Like his nineteenth-century counterpart, Rayber also views himself as a suffering child. He believes that his uncle seduced him as a young boy into believing Christian mythology. As Rayber listens to a missionary child

25. Dostoevsky, *The Brothers Karamazov*, 243, 238.

26. Ibid., 237.

27. Ibid. In the original Russian, the word "надрывом" is repeated twice, the root of which is *nadryv*, a leitmotif Dostoevsky employs throughout the novel. While Pevear translates it as "with the strain of a lie" and drops the repetition, Dostoevsky's version is more intense. In *Reading Dostoevsky*, Victor Terras breaks the word into two pieces: "*nadryv*, derived from *rvat'*, 'to tear,' with the prefix *nad-*, 'over'" (155). Ivan is stressing and repeating his distaste for such love. A more literal translation would read: "I am convinced he did it with lacerating anguish (надрывом), with lacerating/anguished lies (надрывом лжи) . . . ."

28. Dostoevsky, *The Brothers Karamazov*, 236.

29. Ibid.

named Lucette Carmody preach—a girl whom he considers "exploited"—he recalls how his uncle kidnapped him: "He saw himself taking the offered hand and innocently walking out of his own yard, innocently walking into six or seven years of unreality."[30] Rayber repeats the adverb "innocently" to stress how blameless he was and perhaps how corrupted he felt after being baptized by his uncle. Watching Lucette preach, Rayber desires to save all the oppressed of the world, including "himself when he was a child."[31] Rayber's pain comes from his torn desires between believing the Christian argument posed by Old Tarwater and Lucette and living in what he believes is the "real world." O'Connor ranks the suffering "caused by the doubts of those who want to believe" as the highest possible, and therefore deserving of compassion and pity.[32]

Moreover, Rayber deserves pity for the way he received the gospel; his uncle Mason Tarwater had been utterly unaccommodating in teaching him about the things of God.[33] Rayber's parents had rescued him from the prophet's confinement, and they seem to have taught the child that his uncle meant nothing but evil by these abusively "Christian" acts. Yet the seeds "fell in deep," as Mason observes, so that Rayber still regards himself as an innocent waiting to be rescued by Jesus: he feels "as if he were still a child waiting on Christ" and recalls his "childhood pain laid again on his tongue like a bitter wafer," referencing the Eucharist or Christ's bodily suffering, though it tastes "bitter."[34]

In *Things Hidden* literary theorist René Girard stresses that "you cannot see and make visible the truth except by taking the place of the victim [however], you must already be occupying that place."[35] Although Girard's insight clarifies why suffering has been such a catalyst for philosophical insight for so many writers, from Boethius and Dante to Dostoevsky and O'Connor, he is referring here to Christ who was not overcome by the violence of the world but acted contrary to it by bearing it away. Jeremiah Alberg interprets Girard's assessment of Christ as evidence that O'Connor

---

30. O'Connor, *Collected Works*, 408.

31. Ibid., 412.

32. O'Connor, *The Habit of Being*, 353.

33. Old Tarwater worries that "he might have helped the nephew on to his new course" (*Collected Works*, 334). Alberg rightly points out that Tarwater "has to accept the possibility that he had, in fact, scandalized a little one and that he is dependent on the Lord for mercy in light of that sin" (*Beneath the Veil*, 115).

34. O'Connor, *Collected Works*, 443, 412.

35. Girard, *Things Hidden Since the Foundation of the World*, 218–19.

"found the spirit of truth that makes every victim into an *alter Christus*, another Christ."[36] By seeing her personal agony as participation in the pain of Christ, O'Connor could see and make visible the truth about suffering and injustice in the world. However, Rayber rejects any interpretation of his suffering as coterminus with that of Christ. Though his suffering could potentially proffer revelation, Rayber instead chooses blindness. In contrast to their authors, Ivan and Rayber refuse to admit Christ's suffering. They instead employ their misery as fodder against Christ, and thus they remain unenlightened.

In addition to his own despair, Ivan has sought out stories from various travelers and contemporary newspapers about children tormented across the European continent, from the Swiss to the Turks, and even from Russia itself. He does not simply point at the evil of other cultures but indicts his own nation of cruelty: "We have our historical, direct, and intimate delight in the torture of beating."[37] The stories are horrifying, even more so because of their historical reality: Dostoevsky collected these accounts himself.[38] When the censors attempted to remove certain phrases, for instance, from the story of a young girl locked in a privy and "smeared with excrement," Dostoevsky objects that they "mustn't soften it" for the details not only show the impact that these stories have had on Ivan but also potentially will have a similar effect on his readers.[39] One can imagine that Dostoevsky suffered as much reading these accounts as Ivan does in relating them and Alyosha does upon hearing them. Who does not feel pain after Ivan's litany of these tortured little ones?

Yet, Ivan uses these stories to make a move that neither Dostoevsky nor Alyosha can contend with—he lines up this evidence in judgment against God and rules him unjust. After Ivan describes these accounts, he asks Alyosha, "If everyone must suffer in order to buy eternal harmony with their suffering, pray tell me what have children got to do with it? It's

---

36. Alberg, *Beneath the Veil*, 105.

37. Dostoevsky, *The Brothers Karamazov*, 240.

38. Frank, *A Writer in His Time*, 789: "All the tortures that Dostoevsky portrays through Ivan's feverish words were taken from newspaper accounts or from historical sources for which he was ready to give the exact reference."

39. Ibid. Dostoevsky objects to censoring the excrement passage in two different letters. First, he reminds the editors of the audience: "You mustn't soften it . . . . We are not writing for ten-year-old children." Second, he explains about the importance of the details for Ivan's character: "If a twenty-three-year-old notices, that means he took it to heart."

quite incomprehensible why they should suffer, and why they should buy harmony for their suffering."[40] He emphasizes his inability to "comprehend" the disjunction between eternal harmony and earthly suffering. The question seems in earnest, for Ivan repeats it in different forms, as though begging for someone to solve his seemingly unanswerable question. Then, Ivan distinguishes between a rejection of God and that of God's world: "It's not that I don't accept God, you understand, it is the world of God's created by God, that I do not accept."[41] Since Ivan cannot reason through God's purported goodness and this world he created where children suffer, he infamously returns his ticket to eternal harmony.

In *The Violent Bear It Away*, Rayber composes a much shorter list of suffering innocents, including the babies slain by Herod at the coming of Christ, Lucette Carmody, himself, Bishop, and young Tarwater. During Lucette's testimony, she retells the story from Matthew 2:16 in which Herod tries to murder the newborn Jesus by killing all male children under two years old. She contrasts the world's way of reading the story with her own: "The world hoped old Herod would slay the right child, the world hoped old Herod wouldn't waste those children, but he wasted them. He didn't get the right one. Jesus grew up and raised the dead."[42] The passage presents strong evidence against God's goodness, for what God would allow so many helpless toddlers to be slaughtered? Rayber responds with exclamations of disapproval, "But not those dead! he cried, not the innocent children, not you, not me when I was a child, not Bishop, not Frank!"[43] Rayber objects for the same reasons as Ivan; neither accepts eventual resurrection as vindication for these children's death. They are blind and deaf to any other way to perceive these stories.

Girard offers a different paradigm through which to view both Ivan's newspaper accounts and the passage from Matthew. When Girard analyzes literature, he cautions the reader against the temptation to apply "to the work the meanings he already applies to the world."[44] By limiting their perspective to the temporal world, Ivan and Rayber cannot understand the mysteries that exceed the here and now. Alberg demonstrates how to read beneath the surface of difficult texts, such as this one:

40. Dostoevsky, *The Brothers Karamazov*, 244.

41. Ibid., 235.

42. O'Connor, *Collected Works*, 413.

43. Ibid.

44. Girard, *Deceit, Desire, and the Novel*, 16.

What O'Connor saw with piercing clarity is that to hope out of a tenderness divorced from Christ that the Holy Innocents had been spared is to hope against salvation. It is to grant those innocents a longer life on earth at the cost of denying them eternal life. It is to accept death as having the last word.[45]

Because he does not believe in eternal life, Rayber does not value Christ's life more than the babies who were slain. Like Ivan, he cannot see how the promise of resurrection trumps earthly violence.

Moreover, both Ivan and Rayber cast blame in the wrong direction. In Girard's terms, Ivan succumbs to the illusion that the blood of the innocent purchases universal peace. According to Ivan's understanding, humans have consented "to accept their happiness on the unjustified blood of a tortured child."[46] Girard calls this the myth of the "founding murder," in which cultures believe that the murder of the innocent creates harmony among people. Through his study of myths and religions, Girard has seen the repetition of this "founding murder," in which cultures accomplish harmony by the death of a victim. While Ivan rejects this foundation, he mistakenly attributes it to the Christian God, as does Rayber. In his vision of saving the innocent, Rayber sees "himself moving like an avenging angel through the world, gathering up all the children that the Lord, not Herod, had slain."[47] Here, Rayber exhibits "Girardian *misrecognition*," which Alberg asserts "lies at the heart of Rayber's scandal at Jesus."[48] He has placed himself in the position of the divine savior and volitionally mistaken God rather than man as the murderer of these children.

Instead of Jesus, Girard blames this illusion on Satan, "the master of the single victim mechanism,"[49] and distinguishes the foundations of other religions from that of Jesus's Passion. Alyosha reminds his brother of the one whose "innocent blood" was not taken but freely given "for all and

45. Alberg, *Beneath the Veil*, 113.

46. Dostoevsky, *The Brothers Karamazov*, 246.

47. O'Connor, *Collected Works*, 413.

48. Alberg, *Beneath the Veil*, 113.

49. Girard, *I See Satan*, 87. Girard sees this murder at the origin of "not only Cainite cultures but of all human cultures," an extension of his thesis that seems to leave no room for the Holy Spirit to found more redemptive versions of culture. See H. Richard Neibuhr's *Christ and Culture* for an alternative account. However, Girard's theory does explain the beginning of Cainite, or worldly, culture, what Augustine describes as the "City of Man." Moreover, he does well to distance this founding murder from Jesus' passion on the cross.

for everything." Alyosha argues, "[I]t is on Him that the structure is being built."[50] Girard concurs and credits Frederich Nietzsche with explaining how this death opposes the idea of human sacrifice. Nietzsche argues, "Through Christianity, the individual was made so important, so absolute, that he could no longer be *sacrificed*."[51] Although Ivan and Rayber desire to save the victims of the world, they are removing themselves from the opposition to violence, the source of protection, the foundation of individual worth, the only God who suffers, the origin of love itself. And thus, their love is nothing but mere fantasy.

"LOVE IN DREAMS" AND THEORETICAL TENDERNESS

Ivan begins his tirade against God with a frightening admission, "I never could understand how it's possible to love one's neighbors. In my opinion, it is precisely one's neighbors that one cannot possibly love."[52] The word choice "neighbor"[53] evokes the Golden Rule that Jesus lays out in the Gospel, "Love your neighbor as yourself."[54] It should be noted that this rule is second, drawn from the first, which is to "love the Lord your God with all your heart and with all your soul and with all your mind and with all your strength."[55] Jesus says the second rule is like the first one, as though the two rules are entwined. By overthrowing the latter rule, Ivan implies his rejection of the former. He cannot understand the love of neighbors because he cannot understand the love of God.

Alyosha sees that Ivan's love is disingenuous, unreal, and a theoretical embrace of innocent humanity. He refers to Father Zosima's distinction between "любов' мечтательная" ("love in dreams"), on the one hand, which "thirsts for immediate action, quickly performed, and with everyone watching" versus "любов' деятел'ная" ("active love"), on the other, which "is labor and perseverance, and for some people, perhaps, a whole

---

50. Dostoevsky, *The Brothers Karamazov*, 246.

51. Nietzsche, *Will to Power*, 141–42. Quoted in Wolfgang Palaver's *René Girard's Mimetic Theory*, 198.

52. Dostoevsky, *The Brothers Karamazov*, 236.

53. Dostoevsky uses the word "ближнего" for "neighbor," which is the same word used in translations of the New Testament passages in which Jesus uses it.

54. Mark 12:30–31; Matthew 22:36–40.

55. Ibid.

science."[56] Zosima has defined these two terms in response to a woman's confession of the loss of her faith. Although the elder acknowledges that he cannot "prove" God's existence to her, he advises her to participate in active love: "Try to love your neighbors actively and tirelessly. The more you succeed in loving, the more you'll be convinced of the existence of God and the immortality of your soul."[57] Because Ivan cannot comprehend active love, he misses the experiential evidence of God's existence as well as the truth of resurrection. Moreover, Ivan's excitement over the accounts of the suffering children betrays how impersonal his love is for these beings. What repels Ivan also in some way attracts him; he elaborates upon the details when telling the stories to Alyosha: "The main delight comes from doing it before their mother's eyes."[58] To Ivan these children who are tortured are all faceless and held at a distance. He objectifies them as evidence for his protest.

For Ivan, active love is impossible because it would require human beings to be like God. He distrusts the possibility of what he describes as Christlike love: "In my opinion, Christ's love for people is in its kind a miracle impossible on earth. True, he was God. But we are not gods."[59] Ivan draws a sharp line between earthly and human potentialities versus that of God, whom he implies committed impossible acts. Because we are not gods, we are unable to love our flawed neighbors. However, Ivan imagines that he could love children up close because they alone are perfect. Despite his assertion, he never exhibits any love for a child over the course of the novel, and his supposition that children can never be sinful[60] implies a disassociation from reality. While Dostoevsky might echo a similar sentiment, the notion of faultless children defies the orthodox Christian doctrine that human beings are imperfect creatures.

Taking these scenes from *The Brothers Karamazov* as a lens through which to view Rayber reveals much about his misunderstanding of love. When Rayber tries to rationalize his love for Bishop, he cannot do it. For Bishop, he feels "love without reason, love for something futureless, love

56. Dostoevsky, *The Brothers Karamazov*, 58.

57. Ibid., 54.

58. Ibid., 238.

59. Ibid., 237.

60. Dostoevsky uses the word "дурных," which Volokhonsky and Pevear translate as "homely," but that adjective misses the meaning of the word. It can be translated as "bad" or "ugly" or "sinful" or "dark," but "homely" lacks the negative connotations.

that appeared to exist only to be itself, imperious and all demanding."[61] In contrast to Rayber's rationalist definition of love, the kind he uses to solve his difficult psychological cases, the love that Bishop initiates in him is transcendent. He experiences what Zosima refers to as active love. However, rather than turn towards God, Rayber mistrusts the experience and rejects the truths towards which it points. To describe this love, he uses words such as "horrifying," "terrify[ing]," "irrational," "abnormal," and describes it as "an avalanche [that] covered everything his reason hated."[62] Rayber sets himself at odds with this love, threatened by what it conjures in him—a desire to submit to his uncle's vision of the world.

Because of his innocence, Bishop instigates this form of love in Rayber. Though Rayber doubts "that he himself was formed in the image and likeness of God," he sees in Bishop the evidence of the *imago dei*.[63] While Ivan loves at a distance, Rayber loves a suffering child up close and daily. In defiance of this love and the source to which it leads, Rayber initially tries to drown his son. He only ceases to murder Bishop when he realizes that the child not only starts the "pain [of love], he also limit[s] it, contain[s] it."[64] If Rayber loses Bishop, then "the whole world would become his idiot child."[65] This concrete love for every creature of God echoes precisely the teaching of Father Zosima: He preaches that each person is responsible to all and for all, a responsibility that both Ivan and Rayber reject, the former deeming it miraculous, while the latter considers it a sign of God's stupidity. Rayber uses words such as "fool" and "madness" to describe this love.[66] Considering himself an intellectual, Rayber views this type of love, and thus the God from whom it stems, as beneath him.

"WHO ARE YOU?": HUMAN PRIDE VS. OMNIPOTENT GOD

The primary problem at the root of Ivan's and Rayber's objection to God's design is pride. By questioning God's goodness or power, the two rebels assume the right to probe all secrets of the universe. Their assumption

61. O'Connor, *Collected Works*, 401.

62. Ibid.

63. Ibid.

64. Ibid., 418.

65. Ibid., 442.

66. Ibid., 401.

demonstrates a misunderstanding not only of human beings but also of God: the query implies that humans have sufficient reason to comprehend all mystery and simultaneously reduces God to earthly categories of cognition, which eliminates both his divinity and sovereignty. Rather than acknowledge limits in their ability to understand, Ivan and Rayber judge God according to their terms.

Both Ivan and Rayber put too much stock in the human ability to know everything. Ivan feigns humility with Alyosha several times, but his argument betrays his true beliefs. While Ivan attests, "I don't understand anything,"[67] he follows this seemingly Socratic assertion with monologues about the problems with the world and the mistakes in God's system. As though indignant at his position below God, Ivan bitingly calls his ability to reason the "vile concoction of man's Euclidean mind, feeble and puny as an atom" limited by the Creator to "three dimensions of space."[68] While Ivan lays bare an obvious pride in his intellect, he simultaneously laments the potential restrictions to knowledge asserted by Christian mystery, or what he disdainfully refers to as "reasoning from another world."[69] Rayber imitates this confidence in his education in the "real world" in opposition to the visions and biblical recitations of Old Tarwater.[70] "He don't know it's anything he can't know," Mason tells young Tarwater.[71]

In contrast to their characters, Dostoevsky and O'Connor believe that it is foolishness to assume a human being has no limits to knowledge. Dostoevsky writes, "The doctrine that the mind of man is the final limit of the universe is as stupid as stupid can be, and even stupider, infinitely stupider than a game of checkers between two shopkeepers."[72] O'Connor echoes him when she asserts that the "basic experience of everyone is the experience of human limitation."[73] In defiance of this experience, both Ivan and Rayber presume their reason can answer all questions, effectually reducing the world, including theological or supernatural aspects, to empirical, visible reality.

---

67. Dostoevsky, *The Brothers Karamazov*, 243.

68. Ibid., 235.

69. Ibid., 238.

70. O'Connor, *Collected Works*, 375.

71. Ibid., 366.

72. From *Polnoe Sobranie Sochinenii*, vol. 16, quoted in Frank, *Dostoevsky: The Mantle of the Prophet*, 153–54.

73. O'Connor, *Mystery and Manners*, 131.

Several of O'Connor's characters are such "innerleckchuls"[74] who assume that reason is the *only* necessary faculty. For example, Asbury Fox, in "The Enduring Chill," convinces himself of his impending death and invites a Jesuit priest over for his last intellectual repartee. Instead, his mother procures an unsophisticated diocesan priest. When Asbury attempts to debate about Joyce and the myth of a dying god with Father Finn, the priest responds with practical questions to gauge Asbury's purity and knowledge of the catechism. Father Finn asks, "Who is God?" to which Asbury replies, "God is an idea created by man," considering the catechism a game "that two could play at."[75] His answer places him in Ivan's lineage, not to mention Voltaire's and Feuerbach's, among others. In his dialogue with Alyosha, Ivan quotes Voltaire, and declares, "[M]an, has, indeed, invented God."[76] Unlike Ivan, Asbury's assertion is unequivocally denounced by his interlocutor. The priest diagnoses Asbury: "He's a good lad at heart but very ignorant."[77] All of Asbury's learning has not educated him about God, the world, or himself. Though Asbury asserts himself as an extraordinary intellectual, the priest finds his type of intellect useless.

In these stories and in her nonfiction, O'Connor shows that mere ratiocinative intellect is insufficient, for reason should lead beyond knowledge of this world to the greater knowledge of God. She underscores unknowable mystery in her essays on writing: "The fiction writer presents mystery through manners, grace through nature, but when he finishes there always has to be left over that sense of Mystery which cannot be accounted for by any human formula."[78] True reason takes into account radical mystery—what the human being cannot know. As Dr. Block says in "The Enduring Chill," "Most things are beyond me. . . . I ain't found anything yet that I thoroughly understood."[79] Ironically, the doctor, one of the most knowledgeable characters in the story, exhibits the greatest intellectual humility. In contrast to the doctor, Asbury is blinded by his pride. When Dr. Block attempts to diagnose Asbury's illness, Asbury dismisses him, assuming

74. Onnie Jay Holy uses this word to describe Hazel Motes, a thinking but not practicing atheist; he says, "That's the trouble with you innerleckschuls . . . you don't never have nothing to show for what you're saying" (O'Connor, *Collected Works*, 90).

75. O'Connor, *Collected Works*, 566.

76. Dostoevsky, *The Brothers Karamazov*, 234.

77. O'Connor, *Collected Works*, 567.

78. O'Connor, *Mystery and Manners*, 153.

79. O'Connor, *Collected Works*, 557.

his oncoming death is beyond Block's comprehension. Asbury's mother recognizes her son's blindness: "When people think they are smart—even when they are smart—there is nothing anybody else can say to make them see things straight."[80] Only after Dr. Block correctly diagnoses Asbury's illness as undulant fever, does Asbury begin to realize his own blindness and limitation.

Asbury's mother's words prove even more accurate in the case of Ivan and Rayber, who refuse to admit any truth beyond their perspective. When the doctor explains Bishop's condition to Rayber, he attempts to comfort him with descriptions of more deformed children, to which Rayber responds in fury, "'How can I be grateful,' he had hissed,[81] 'when one—just one—is born with a heart outside?'"[82] Rayber echoes Ivan who asks Alyosha, would you found a world on which all people were happy but one child must beat its breast with her little fist?[83] Alyosha concedes Ivan's point, but Rayber's uncle is a less sympathetic listener. When Rayber demands, "Ask the Lord why he made [Bishop] an idiot in the first place," Mason shouts in response, "Yours not to ask! . . . Yours not to question the mind of the Lord God Almighty. Yours not to grind the Lord into your head and spit out a number!"[84] Here, Mason connects Rayber's pride with his dependence on reductive reason. Although Ivan's and Rayber's doubts appear reasonable, their questions of God's goodness exceed human limitations.

Moreover, their questions make demands of God. They echo Mrs. Ruby Turpin from O'Connor's "Revelation" who yells at God, "Who do you think you are?"[85] Mrs. Turpin is a farmer's wife who undergoes a revelation about her place in the universe when a young girl strikes her and calls her a warthog from hell. The insult contradicts her self-image as a middle-class, God-fearing white woman. She asks God, "How am I a hog and me both? How am I saved and from hell too?"[86] The young girl's blow forces Mrs. Turpin to confront her pride, and in a fury, she cries out to God, "Who do

80. Ibid., 550.

81. The verb "hiss," a sound mimicking a serpent, points to the latent demonism in Rayber. Though O'Connor did not want to conflate Rayber with the devil, he espouses demonic claims throughout the novel.

82. O'Connor, *Collected Works*, 416.

83. Dostoevsky, *The Brothers Karamazov*, 245; Ursula LeGuin writes a story based on this premise called "The Ones Who Walk Away from Omelas."

84. O'Connor, *Collected Works*, 351.

85. Ibid., 653.

86. Ibid., 652.

you think you are?"[87] This question echoes Job from the Old Testament, the archetype of the doubting sufferer. Susan Srigley notes, "Ruby is like Job in that she is more interested in her question as to why the righteous suffer, than in God's question—Why are the righteous pious?"[88] The characters that presume that they are righteous have rivaled God's authority by believing that the human being is "good" enough to question God.

Ivan and Rayber are not only emboldened by their assumptions of righteousness and presumed intellectual superiority but also by their miscomprehension of the Judeo-Christian God that they reject. Ivan's heresies, which he illustrates in his poem "The Legend of the Grand Inquisitor," are inherited by Rayber a century later. Although scholars debate whether the Christ character in Ivan's poem would have been applauded or derided by Dostoevsky himself and whether or not this figure represents the historical personage described in the Gospel accounts, it is my contention that Ivan's Christ is an aberration, an example of how Ivan misunderstands God and why he easily dismisses him as ineffectual.

MONOPHYSITE CHRIST

"The Legend of the Grand Inquisitor" is one of the most famous passages penned by Dostoevsky, sometimes even published separately from *The Brothers Karamazov*. The chapter occurs directly following Ivan's protest on behalf of the suffering children and precedes Alyosha's hagiography of Zosima, which runs counter to both the "Rebellion" and the Inquisitor poem. Yet Ivan wrote the poem, and it expresses his philosophy, not Dostoevsky's. In creating this Christ character, Ivan enacts his belief that men have made God in their image. Ivan feigns to evade the debate over who created whom, as he tells Alyosha, "As for me, I've long resolved not to think whether man created God or God man."[89] However, by sidestepping the issue, Ivan by default declares "man's" preeminence.

In "The Legend of the Grand Inquisitor," Ivan depicts a fabricated deity who is nothing but mankind's invention. O'Connor recognizes how this

87. The conclusion elaborates upon Mrs. Turpin, considering her connection to Job. Through Mrs. Turpin, O'Connor shows how God answers the rebel's question with revelation, a point that is not within the scope of this chapter.

88. Srigley, *Flannery O'Connor's Sacramental Art*, 152. Srigley acknowledges that J. Gerald Janzen makes this point in *Job*, 2.

89. Dostoevsky, *The Brothers Karamazov*, 216.

evaluation alters people's actions. She addresses the change in novelistic terms:

> It makes a great difference to [a] novel whether [the novelist] believes that we are created in God's image, or whether he [or she] believes we create God in our own. It makes a great difference whether he [or she] believes that our wills are free, or bound like those of other animals.[90]

In the same way that a novelist's understanding of reality affects the course of a story, so a character's notion of who created whom determines his or her actions. If the human being created God, then God is limited to human comprehension, and such a domesticated God becomes a means to each person's goals.

Though Ivan hesitates to say that humans created God, the nineteenth-century philosopher Friedrich Nietzsche is unabashed in accusing Christians of worshipping a god of human invention. Nietzsche protests that the church "*created* its 'God' according to its needs" and he accuses Christians of a lack of holiness:

> Possessing even the tiniest bit of piety in the body, we should find a god who cures a cold at the right time or who bids us enter a coach at the very moment when a violent rainstorm begins, such an absurd god that we should have to abolish him if he existed.[91]

This "god" is similar to what Ralph Wood calls the "parking-place Jesus," who magically finds Christians parking places close to shop entrances.[92] Such a God is the figment of human creation, a guise for the self-will of the individual. If this God is as Nietzsche depicts him, then he should be dismissed.

For Nietzsche, Christians are the ultimate nihilists because they follow this God who reigns over nothing in the real world. "The Christian conception of God—God as the god of the sick, God as a spider, God as spirit—is one of the most corrupt conceptions of the divine ever attained on earth. . . . God as the declaration of war against life, against nature,

90. O'Connor, *Mystery and Manners*, 157.

91. Nietzsche, *Portable Nietzsche*, 604, 636.

92. Wood writes, "The false god of the false gospel of religious good works turns out to be someone rather like Santa Clause [who] supposedly gives his followers whatever they want. . . . I have conservative Christian students who tell me that they pray for God to find them a parking place, and that this God of theirs always comes through" (from "By Grace Alone").

against the will to live!"[93] Nietzsche's version of the Christian God is merely a spirit who wages war against everything human, natural, and enjoyable: his depiction should recall Ivan's Christ. Nietzsche admired Dostoevsky, and it would not be surprising if he drew his own descriptions of God from Ivan's rendition of Christ.[94]

Unlike the historical Jesus who is born to Mary and Joseph in the town of Bethlehem, is raised in Nazareth, and dies in Jerusalem, Ivan's Christ arrives from nowhere. Like a spirit, he comes "quietly, inconspicuously" and "passes silently among them with a quiet smile of infinite compassion."[95] He seems incorporeal and unreal. Ivan increases this effect by describing him in unearthly terms: "The sun of love shines in His heart, rays of Light, Enlightenment, and Power stream from His eyes, and pouring over the people, shake their hearts with responding love."[96] These poetic metaphors portray Christ as a docetic figure devoid of any human aspect. As a poet, Ivan knows how to depict characters: his Inquisitor is fully embodied, vividly depicted as "an old man, almost ninety, tall and straight, with a gaunt face and sunken eyes, from which a glitter still shines like a fiery spark. . . . At this moment, he is wearing only his old, coarse monastic cassock."[97] Ivan describes his specific age, the lines of his face, and even his current ensemble. This second Christ, by contrast, is only spirit, fleshless and thus, unable to answer the Grand Inquisitor's hard charges.

In addition to lacking place, this Christ has no family, no disciples, and most importantly, no Trinitarian identity. This Christ calls no one to follow him; he performs a few nondescript miracles and says a handful of imperative words in conjunction with these acts before the Inquisitor imprisons him. Then, after listening to the Inquisitor's impressive monologue, he responds with a kiss that "burns in [the Inquisitor's] heart, but the old man holds to his former idea."[98] Finding himself unnecessary to the people,

---

93. Nietzsche, *Portable Nietzsche*, 585.

94. Numerous books have been written connecting Dostoevsky and Nietzsche. In an 1888 letter to Georg Brandes, for example, Nietzsche writes, "Dostoevski; I prize his work . . . as the most valuable psychological material known to me—I am grateful to him in a remarkable way, however much he goes against my deepest instincts" (from *Selected Letters*, 327). Despite their oppositional conclusions about God, Nietzsche found a kinship with Dostoevsky.

95. Dostoevsky, *The Brothers Karamazov*, 249.

96. Ibid.

97. Ibid.

98. Ibid., 262.

Christ leaves. This Christ makes no impression upon this community because it does not need him—the people have the Inquisitor.

"The Legend of the Grand Inquisitor" depicts Christ as Ivan sees him and the Inquisitor as a reflection of Ivan himself. After the poem has ended, Alyosha draws the connections between Ivan and his brother, accusing both of not believing in God.[99] The way that Ivan describes the Inquisitor reveals how he sees himself, as "one sufferer who is tormented by a great sadness and loves mankind."[100] While Ivan identifies himself as a sufferer and lover of mankind, he does not recognize Christ as the predecessor of this suffering and the source of love. The choice is compelled by the "directives of the intelligent spirit" which one must follow even if it means "accept[ing] lies and deceit" and leading people to "death and destruction."[101] Rather than imitate Christ and see his own suffering as participation with the one who suffered, Ivan believes his choice is between self-destruction or the deception and annihilation of others. Ivan's trust in his intellect has led him to create an idol in the Grand Inquisitor, an idol that sounds a lot like the one who was a liar and a murderer from the beginning.[102]

Rayber easily puts this Gnostic god to death and subsumes his role. For Rayber, Christ is the figment of his uncle's imagination, a crutch he leans on and uses to justify his life choices. He accuses his uncle of "calling himself" into the ministry, assuming that Old Tarwater's God is of his own making. Rayber attempts to unveil what he assumes to be is a façade: "You've got to be born again, Uncle . . . by your own efforts, back to the real world where there's no saviour but yourself."[103] While Rayber employs religious language, the words are meaningless, or rather subjective; they mean whatever he desires them to mean. When Rayber begins to raise the young Tarwater as his son, he tries to undo the teachings of his uncle, beginning first with the superficial nonsense of the resurrection. Coming

99. Ibid., 261–62: Alyosha exclaims, "Your Inquisitor doesn't believe in God" and later says to Ivan, "You don't believe in God." When Ivan concludes the poem with the kiss that glows in his Inquisitor's heart, though he adheres to his ideas, Alyosha exclaims, "And you with him!" Then, Alyosha imitates Christ by kissing Ivan, again linking Ivan with his character.

100. Ibid., 261.

101. Ibid., 262.

102. Girard reiterates this in *Resurrection*: "The diabolical choice of the Inquisitor is nothing else than a reflection of the diabolical choice made by Ivan Karamazov" (66). This will be elaborated upon in chapter 3.

103. O'Connor, *Collected Works*, 379.

upon a sign that speaks of being "born again" and "eternal life," Rayber informs Tarwater that people will not rise again: "That's why I want you to learn. I want you to be educated so that you can take your place as an intelligent man in the world."[104] Rayber begins Tarwater's instruction by removing any knowledge of a transcendent reality and placing education and human intelligence as the highest end. Following in the footsteps of Ivan, Rayber tries to undress the myth of the supernatural Christ, so the autonomous individual is the bare reality.

CORRECTING CHRIST'S WORK: FROM THE GRAND INQUISITOR TO THE DISPLACED PERSON

With such a demoted view of Christ, Ivan and Rayber commence their projects to rival God's authority. After subjugating him to fiction or to a worthless myth, he is ineffectual for the problems in the world. Therefore, they take the burden upon themselves to improve the deficiencies that they find abounding. The Grand Inquisitor, the mouthpiece of Ivan, informs Christ that he has "corrected" his work.[105] And, Rayber defies the resurrection in preference for humanism, as he teaches Tarwater, "The great dignity of man . . . is his ability to say: I am born once and no more. What I can see and do for myself and fellowman in this life is all of my portion and I'm content with it."[106] In opposition to Christ's kingdom, they establish alternative orders of religion with their selves as the gods. Against the grand plans of their characters, Dostoevsky and O'Connor show how any kingdom but that of Christ is one of violence, to use Girard's language. In his discussions of the gospel, Girard maintains the "ambiguity and ubiquity of violence," that even those who attempt to renounce violence, if apart from following Christ, will commit further violence.[107]

The Grand Inquisitor exemplifies Girard's theory. The day before Christ's return, the Inquisitor has burned a hundred heretics at the stake—violence in the name of keeping peace and reducing suffering for the people. Though the Grand Inquisitor rules in the name of Christ, he does not believe in his efficacy. The source of Ivan's Grand Inquisitor can be seen

104. Ibid., 399.

105. Dostoevsky, *The Brothers Karamazov*, 260.

106. O'Connor, *Collected Works*, 437.

107. Girard, *Things Hidden*, 198.

historically in the Christian Socialists in late nineteenth-century Russia. Instead of finding their roots in the Russian Orthodox Church, the Russian youth became elated by the European visions of social progress. They read European novels by Fourier and Dickens that promoted social aid. Jesus was appropriated as the humanist icon for socialist reform. Instead of following Christ, they used him as a figurehead for their own agenda. When Alyosha denounces the Inquisitor as an atheist, he voices Dostoevsky's similar condemnation of Christian socialism as atheistic. In *The Devils*, Dostoevsky explores the manifold violence such atheist reformers will cause. Dostoevsky died before he saw the Russian socialists overthrow the czar, kill off his family, and rob the Orthodox Church of all bank credits and land holdings. While Dostoevsky thought that no human being would relinquish his or her freedom for these utopian visions, twentieth-century Russians proved him, for the first time, unprophetic.

Dostoevsky and O'Connor are not the first to illustrate the ways that human pride and the desire to correct God's imperfect world may perpetuate violence. In her "Introduction to a Memoir of Mary Ann," O'Connor cites Nathaniel Hawthorne's 1848 short story "The Birthmark" in which the scientist Alymer, in his attempt to improve his wife's face by erasing her birthmark, unintentionally takes her life. O'Connor reads the story allegorically, knowing that some will see the cancerous Mary Ann with her bulging eye tumor as "the visible mark of earthly imperfection," to use Hawthorne's words.[108] Moreover, O'Connor does not underestimate her audience; she knows that there are those who will ask why Mary Ann should have ever been born,[109] a question Rayber posits about his son Bishop. To Tarwater, Rayber idealizes a future in which "people may have learned enough to put [children such as Bishop or Mary Ann] to sleep when they're born."[110] O'Connor's word choice, "learned enough," reminds readers of where Rayber places his trust—in the human intellect. He would have applauded Alymer for undertaking such a heroic task without conceding the tragedy of the wife's death.

The eugenics movement materialized O'Connor's fears. In the 1920s and 1930s, America led the way in the eugenics movement, outdoing even

---

108. O'Connor, *Collected Works*, 823; O'Connor does not give Hawthorne's passage a citation.

109. Ibid., 830.

110. Ibid., 435.

Germany in its number of procedures. Ian Dowbiggin catalogues eugenics' effect on America:

> Most of America's geneticists, biologists, physicians, and social scientists embraced eugenics, a trend that culminated in the founding of the American Eugenics Society (AES) in 1923. Eugenics pervaded college, university and high school curricula. The Carnegie and Rockefeller Foundations funded eugenic research. Eugenics seeped into popular culture, too, evident in the "better baby contests" and numerous movies and stage dramas about the dangers of sexually transmitted diseases.[111]

The acceptance of eugenics across the American landscape cannot be exaggerated. Only Roman Catholic theologians and scientists seem to have spoken out against it. In 1930 Pope Pius XI denounced the practice in his encyclical *Casti Connubii* on Christian marriage, but only when the horrors of the Third Reich became public did eugenicists themselves become wary of the moral problems with forced sterilization.

In conjunction with the eugenics movement, the birth control movement in the 1920s fulfilled these expectations, aiming to better society. According to Margaret Sanger, these movements should work in conjunction to rid society of the "unfit," which included those poverty-stricken, mentally challenged, or suffering from tuberculosis, gonorrhea, syphilis, cancer, epilepsy, insanity, drunkenness, or mental disorders. Anyone with these afflictions should not produce children, and Sanger makes a list of criteria for those who should or should not have children. In an editorial on the eugenic resolution, she writes (March 13, 1925), "We claim that all children who are brought into this world *must* give promise of being of value to the community, and that if there is any doubt or indication to the contrary, in the traits of heredity, such possible parents must refrain from exercising the function of parenthood."[112] Birth control, for Sanger, aids in preventing the birth of invaluable children and assures that only the best specimens of the population are breeding.

Many birth control and eugenics advocates feared they would be connected to the eugenics movement of the Third Reich, for the terminology of both groups sound hauntingly similar. According to Dowbiggin, American eugenicists initially hailed Nazi sterilization laws "as a step in the right direction," only drawing back when "the racial overtones of Hitler's policies

111. Dowbiggin, *The Sterilization Movement*, 25.

112. Sanger, "Editorial on the Eugenic Resolution."

became more and more evident."[113] While American eugenicists avoided racial sterilization laws, they did not observe a parallel in their procedures on the mentally challenged. However, the American and Nazi eugenicists shared the same agenda—to counteract the production of what they considered weak individuals.

Farrell O'Gorman delineates the effects of the eugenics movement on O'Connor's consciousness, beginning with her proximity to the State Hospital in her hometown Milledgeville, which was the center of Georgia's eugenic activity. He also mentions her "Introduction to a Memoir of Mary Ann," in which she states her horror of those "busy cutting down human imperfection."[114] While O'Gorman does not claim that O'Connor actively engages in opposing eugenics, he observes in her fiction an apprehension about the suffering caused by those who attempt to improve society. He gives ample evidence from several of her stories, where characters obsess about their genetics, then he concludes *The Violent Bear It Away* with: "While Rayber is not a eugenicist per se, his broadly eugenic anxieties regarding his (and all humanity's) apparently flawed blood—watch how many times that word appears in the novel—are ultimately bound up with his desire to euthanize his own child."[115] Not only does Rayber attempt to drown Bishop, but also he anticipates a time when human beings will abort such "idiots" before they are delivered.

In all of her works dealing with this problem, O'Connor underlines the rejection of God as the root of the problem. Written prior to *The Violent Bear It Away*, "The Displaced Person" ties the atrocities of the Holocaust to the dismissal of Jesus, the ultimate "displaced person." Fleeing from Nazi Germany, a Polish family called the Guizacs takes refuge in the South on Mrs. McIntyre's farm. From the moment they arrive, they are treated by everyone as outcasts, especially the hired hand Mr. Guizac. Although they recently escaped a society that desired their deaths, the Guizacs do not find America to be any different, which is O'Connor's point. The genocide occurring "over there" was always a possibility here, for it is the result of human failing. In this story, she indicts her fellow Southerners. For instance, Mrs. Shortley, the wife of one of Mrs. McIntyre's attendants, dehumanizes the Guizacs when she first perceives them: "Every time she had seen them in her imagination, the image she had got was of the three bears, walking

113. Dowbiggin, *Sterilization*, 27.

114. O'Connor, *Collected Works*, 830.

115. O'Gorman, "'A dry and seedless fruit,'" 10.

single file, with wooden shoes on like Dutchmen and sailor hats and bright coats with a lot of buttons."[116] As an outsider, Mr. Guizac becomes a target for violence.

O'Connor directly ties Mrs. Shortley's blindness to that of the Nazis abroad. Mrs. Shortley associates these "invading" Polish refugees with news footage of the holocaust, as a means both of distancing these images of dead naked bodies from her but also associating the Guizacs with them:

> Mrs. Shortley had the sudden intuition that the Gobblehooks, like rats with typhoid fleas, could have carried all those murderous ways over the water with them directly to this place. If they had come from where that kind of thing was done to them, who was to say they were not the kind that would also do it to others?[117]

Mrs. Shortley casts "murderous ways" onto the outsiders rather than perceiving them within herself. Instead of empathizing with the victims, she transforms them into the murderers and sees herself as a potential victim. Her veritable *reductio ad absurdum* sparks the contagion that will infest all those on Mrs. McIntyre's farm.

Mrs. McIntyre participates in a similar reduction of the Guizacs from fellow sufferers to objects for her use. She conceives of the Guizacs as an investment for the good of her farm, not as refugees who need her help. Her motivation becomes clear when she exclaims to the priest who arranged this setup: "[Mr. Guizac]'s extra and he's upset the balance around here . . . and I'm a logical practical woman and there are no ovens here and no camps and no Christ Our Lord."[118] Her protest recalls the logical and practical purpose of the camps—discarding those extra people who had upset the balance in Germany. Her denial of Christ becomes intimately tied in this statement with her dismissal of Mr. Guizac, for both are useless and inconvenient to Mrs. McIntyre.

Speaking on another plane, the priest tries to reveal reality to Mrs. McIntyre. She denies the horror of the holocaust and denounces Christ, to which the priest moans, "The ovens and the boxcars and the sick children . . . and our dear Lord."[119] The priest considers the suffering abroad as realities that affect him emotionally and which are intimately connected to the suffering of Christ. Yet, Mrs. McIntyre denies such a spiritual connection in

116. O'Connor, *Collected Works*, 286.

117. Ibid., 287.

118. Ibid., 322.

119. Ibid.

favor of theory, as she tells the priest, "I'm not theological. I'm practical!"[120] Mrs. McIntyre chooses between two frameworks: the theological that would have moral claim on her and the practical that allows her to dismiss her obligation to Mr. Guizac. She absolves herself: "It's not my responsibility that Mr. Guizac has nowhere to go . . . . I don't find myself responsible for all the extra people in the world."[121] Mrs. McIntyre refuses to see Christ in Mr. Guizac, and thus she sides with the Nazis who classified him as an "extra" person, unnecessary and detrimental to their vision of the ideal society.

Although Mrs. McIntyre does not implement a "final solution," her refusal to accept responsibility for Mr. Guizac leads to his death. When a tractor threatens to crush Mr. Guizac, Mrs. McIntyre refrains from offering him any caution:

> [S]he had started to shout to the Displaced Person but that she had not. She felt her eyes and Mr. Shortley's eyes and the Negro's eyes come together in one look that froze them in collusion forever, and she had heard the little noise the Pole made as the tractor wheel broke his backbone.[122]

As Mrs. McIntyre watches the tractor crush Mr. Guizac, she refers to him as the "Displaced Person" and the "Pole" and not by name.[123] Her complicity in his death began when she ignored her responsibility to him as a fellow human being, one, it should be noted, with an immortal soul. Through "The Displaced Person," O'Connor illustrates the mimetic nature of violence and identifies its root as the repudiation of God.

The death of Mr. Guizac prefigures Bishop's drowning in *The Violent Bear It Away*: both have been cast off as outsiders, extraneous to the good of society, and those who should care for them are complicit in allowing for their deaths. As Rayber awaits Bishop's murder, he exalts himself for his indifference: "It seemed to him that this indifference was the most that human dignity could achieve."[124] When he hears his son struggling against his murderer, Rayber suppresses all emotion, forcing himself not to cry out. Although Rayber uplifts the dignity of humanity, by founding it on a source other than Christ, he loses that same humanity in the process. In

120. Ibid., 316.
121. Ibid., 317.
122. Ibid., 326.
123. She reduces Sulk in the same manner.
124. O'Connor, *Collected Works*, 454.

O'Connor's earlier manuscript, Rayber smiles[125] when Bishop dies, indicating Rayber's sinister appreciation of violence. However, in the final edition of the novel, instead of smiling, Rayber feels nothing: "[I]t was not until he realized there would be no pain that he collapsed."[126] This ending is superior to the first not only for its ambiguity in regards to whether the narrator condemns Rayber but also for its representation of reality. For the large majority of us, it is not sinister gruesomeness or the rages of a serial killer, but apathy and indifference that are the most common culprits of violence.

The title of O'Connor's work alludes to the theme of violence and the implicit presence of Jesus to whom it refers, the one who bears the violence away. In the Gospel accounts, Jesus descends to earth to establish a kingdom of peace and nonviolence, only to suffer crucifixion by the very people whom he came to serve. By Girard's reading, the Passion narrative reveals the pervasiveness of the mimetic contagion. When human beings try to bring about peace, we use violence, whereas the divine suffers it at our hands. His sacrifice proves our need of him. In Girard's theory, this sacrificial victim is called the scapegoat, and his expulsion deludes the community into believing they have rid themselves of evil. In various religions, the victim is a marginal figure, such as a slave, child, or even animal, someone both within and outside of the community.[127] As a surrogate victim, Jesus was both an insider and an outsider. St. John tells us, "He came to that which was his own, but his own did not receive him."[128] Human and divine, servant yet rightful king, holy wise but worldly idiot, Christ exemplifies Girard's notions of a sacred sacrifice.

For O'Connor, Bishop is this Christ symbol, an idea she takes from Dostoevsky via Romano Guardini. In 1956 O'Connor read Guardini's analysis of Dostoevsky's *The Idiot* in which he posits the protagonist of the novel as a genuine Christ figure. She had read *The Idiot* several years before.[129] Whether O'Connor agreed completely with Guardini, she recommended this piece to Betty Hester before describing her own work: "In my novel I have a child—the schoolteacher's boy—whom I aim to have a kind of

125. Driggers, *The Manuscripts of Flannery O'Connor at Georgia College*, 110, 189f 117–33, chapter 6, photocopy, T. em O'C, T, ms.

126. O'Connor, *Collected Works*, 456.

127. Girard, *Violence and the Sacred*, 269–71.

128. John 1:11 (NIV).

129. O'Connor relates a humorous anecdote about her mother picking up her copy of *The Idiot* in a letter in *The Habit of Being*, 56.

redemptive figure."[130] Years later she calls Bishop a "necessary" idiot, though a "very nice unobjectionable idiot."[131] Bishop is not a character to be thrown away. For young Tarwater, Bishop is a stumbling block because he has been called to baptize the boy while another part of his nature, which is under demonic possession, desires to murder him. For Rayber, Bishop is both evidence of God's image and thus of God's stupidity or lack of goodness. Before even beginning to write *The Violent Bear It Away*, O'Connor acknowledges, "I believe and the Church teaches that God is as present in the idiot boy as in the genius."[132] Bishop is as necessary as Mary Ann, for both confront the godless world not with idiocy and suffering—though sometimes that's all the blind are able to see—but with the reality of God.

---

130. O'Connor, *The Habit of Being*, 191.

131. Ibid., 301. The latter adjectives may be contrasting with Dostoevsky's pathetic and contestable figure from the aforementioned novel.

132. O'Connor, *The Habit of Being*, 99.

CHAPTER 2

THE DEATH OF GOD AND THE KINGDOM OF VIOLENCE

IN 1965, ONLY A year after Flannery O'Connor's death, *TIME* magazine ran an article on Christian atheism, but without O'Connor's prophetic irony. The article focuses not on the philosophy of non-Christian thinkers but on the theology promoted by academic scholars in major universities across America.[1] These theologians accept the death of God and compose a theology—despite the contradiction of terms—based on this assumption. The *TIME* author writes:

> The death-of-God theologians do not argue merely that Christianity's traditional "image" of the Creator is obsolete. They say that it is no longer possible to think about or believe in a transcendent God who acts in human history, and that Christianity will have to survive, if at all, without him.[2]

O'Connor parodied these ideas before they were en vogue in her first novel *Wise Blood* in which her "Christian *malgré lui*" establishes the "Church without Christ."[3] And, a century prior, Dostoevsky shows that Christianity without God has been the trend at least as far back as the Spanish

---

1. Such as Thomas J. J. Altizer of Emory University, Paul van Buren of Temple University, William Hamilton of Colgate Rochester Divinity School, and Gabriel Vahanian of Syracuse University.

2. "The 'God is Dead' Movement," *TIME* (Oct. 22, 1965).

3 O'Connor, *Collected Works*, 61

Inquisition. However, instead of survival, these two writers reveal that once God has been dethroned, idols reign and violence spreads.

Both authors represent the death of God through the parricidal impulses of their characters. Figuratively, the parricide is a violent enactment as well as an emblem of deicide. Girard describes parricide thus: "The son desires what the father desires. The pride of the father thwarts the son and, in so doing fortifies his pride in turn. Parricide, the crime of the son-slave committed against a tyrant father, thus comes into view as the underground tragedy par excellence."[4] The mimetic desire to be like the father morphs into a rivalry with the father. Girard views it as simultaneously murder and suicide because of the intimate connection between the father and son. This relationship parallels that with the divine creator in whose image we are made: we desire to achieve the *imago dei* but can do so by trying to become the model rather than represent it. Moreover, in an effort to project ourselves as autonomous individuals, we necessitate the disposal of those who begot us. Thus, the rejection of supernatural authority or metaphysical origin corresponds with the rebellion against earthly authority and origin.

DOSTOEVSKY'S PROPHECY

The Brothers Karamazov begins with an announcement of the "dark and tragic death" of Fyodor Pavlovich Karamazov.[5] The death of the father is not the culmination of the novel because it is not the dramatic climax. Rather, his murder acts as a probing question for the characters as well as for readers about who would desire his death and why. At least three, if not all four, brothers desire their father's death: the eldest Dmitry is in a mimetic rivalry with his father over the affections of Grushenka and Dmitry's inheritance while Ivan, the middle son, finds his father odious and has publicly celebrated a stance for amorality that permits their half-brother Smerdyakov to murder Fyodor. Only Alyosha appears innocent of desiring their father's blood.

While Fyodor Pavlovich deserves no equanimity with the God, he metaphorically represents the Divine Father. In Dostoevsky's nonfiction writing, he condemns Russian fathers like Fyodor who demean the role of father by neglecting their children and falsely represent the Father. In July-August 1877 editions of *The Diary of a Writer*, Dostoevsky criticizes

4. Girard, *Resurrection from the Underground*, 57.

5. Dostoevsky, *The Brothers Karamazov*, 7.

the acquittal of the Dzhunkovsky couple who abused their children. He recognizes that no law condemns a "father's laziness, incompetence, and heartlessness in raising his children," for if such a law existed, "we would have to condemn half of Russia—more than half in fact."[6] These fathers are producing wicked children who have no saving memory from child-hood to which they can cling as they age and mature. "Such children will find it difficult, if not impossible, to accumulate any of the 'sacred memories' that will enable them to navigate later amidst the dangerous shoals of life's temptations."[7] Dostoevsky elaborates on this conviction of "sacred memories" at the conclusion of *The Brothers Karamazov* when Alyosha advises the schoolchildren to remember their shared moment around Ilyusha's tombstone.

Whether Dostoevsky himself had these memories is debatable: Girard draws connections between Dostoevsky's novelistic creation and his biography, assuming that Dostoevsky's father Mikhail Andreevich inspires the character of Fyodor. Tying this father with the political czar, Girard writes: "Ashamed of being Russian, ashamed of being the son of his father, ashamed of being Feodor Mikhailovich Dostoevsky, it is all this accumulated shame that is aired, ventilated, and dissipated in the grand inspired breath of *The Brothers Karamazov*."[8] Though Girard denounces elements of Freud's reading of Dostoevsky, he does not hesitate to psychoanalyze the author himself and "share Freud's sentiments."[9] According to Freud, each son desires to displace the father, who is a rival for him. He writes, "[T]he boy wants to be in his father's place because he admires him and wants to be like him, and also because he wants to put him out of the way."[10] While Freud's description of the "Oedipus complex" sounds similar to Girard's definition of mimetic rivalry, Freud develops his theory differently. The desire to become the father does not stem from the son's mimetic nature but is rooted in a fear of castration. The father threatens the son's masculinity, so the son must annihilate the obstacle that his father poses. For Freud, the parricide in *The Brothers Karamazov* is autobiographically con-

6. Quoted in Frank, *Dostoevsky: The Mantle of the Prophet*, 297: From *Polnoe Sobranie Sochinenii*, 25.

7. Ibid., 246–47.

8. Girard, *Resurrection*, 59.

9. Girard, "Dostoevsky's Demons," 31–34: he says that Freud's essay "Dostoevsky and Parricide" "is more against its subject than about him."

10. Freud, "Dostoevsky and Parricide."

fessional because Dostoevsky desired to murder his father: "We can safely say that Dostoevsky never got free from the feelings of guilt arising from his intention of murdering his father."[11] According to Freud, Dostoevsky's fear of his father led to sadism, gambling, and even epilepsy, as forms of self-punishment. Moreover, Dostoevsky could not escape the political and religious ramifications of his complex relationship with his father: first, he submitted entirely to "his Little Father, the Tsar" and second, "he wavered . . . between faith and atheism."[12] Freud credits Dostoevsky's great intellect for allowing him the possibility of atheism, but ultimately his filial guilt spurred him to become more religious.

Though Freud's article is full of shortcomings,[13] he does astutely connect the familial father to its larger significance in the political and religious fathers. In *The Brothers Karamazov* Dostoevsky portrays the domestic family as a microcosm of the larger world family, emphasizing the necessity of the father-son relationship in various spheres—religion, politics, and of course, the home. For instance, Zosima acts as a father to those in the monastery, and Alyosha acts similarly towards the schoolboys. In nonfictional pieces, Dostoevsky refers to the Tsar as the Father of the Russians, and "that the relation of the Russian people to their Tsar-Father is lovingly free and *without fear*."[14] All of these spheres overlap and interact for Dostoevsky, and the disintegration of the family begins with a poor father-child relationship that affects the accord within the home as well as within the rest of society.

Furthermore, Freud shows the primacy of the father in every life. When *The Brothers Karamazov* existed in planning stages, Dostoevsky referred to it as *Fathers and Children* and titled the intended sequel *Children*, in which the children characters "of the preceding novels would come forward as the main heroes."[15] Dostoevsky's final novel, then, in attempting to answer these large questions about fathers and children, begins with an assessment of the father. Although Fyodor Karamazov is a wretched father in almost every regard, his sons nonetheless owe their existence to him. Indeed, his problematic and non-exemplary character becomes an ironic

---

11. Ibid., 106.

12. Ibid.

13. Frank has an appendix on Freud's article "Dostoevsky and Parricide," where he proves Freud's research factually inaccurate about Dostoevsky's life. *Dostoevsky: The Seeds of Revolt*, 379–91.

14. Ibid., 481.

15. Frank, *Dostoevsky: The Mantle of the Prophet*, 518.

paradigm for belief in God the Father whose ways, as Isaiah declares, are not our ways, whose thoughts are not our thoughts (Isa 55:8).

Though the novel introduces the son Alyosha Karamazov as the subject of the first sentence, he is identified by his relationship to Fyodor, and the paragraph is then devoted not to the son but to the father. Dostoevsky's narrator depicts Fyodor as a senseless buffoon "more naïve and simple-hearted"[16] than wicked, but nevertheless a neglectful father and boastful sensualist. The narrator addresses the reader, "You can easily imagine what a father such a man would be and how he would bring up his children. His behavior as a father was exactly what might be expected."[17] Fyodor's fatherhood, or lack thereof, is the starting point of the novel's conflict.

After neglecting his first son Dmitry, Fyodor remarries and fathers two more children, Ivan and Alyosha, both of whom he characteristically neglects. All three children are initially raised by Grigory the servant, until Fyodor's mother-in-law saves Ivan and Alyosha from their dire circumstances. "Seeing at the first glance that they were unwashed and in dirty linen," she carts the children away from Grigory's care.[18] Grigory considers the children "orphans," and rightly so since their father forgets their existence and easily consents to their removal. Ivan grows up knowing that he and Alyosha "were living not in their own home but on other people's charity, and that their father was a man of whom it was disgraceful to speak."[19] Both boys receive proper care and education from surrogates, but during childhood, they never contact their biological father. The narrator insists, "It must be noted that [Ivan] did not even attempt to communicate with his father, perhaps from pride, from contempt for him, or perhaps from his cool common sense, which told him that from such a father he would get no real assistance."[20] Thus, the Karamazov sons grow up as abandoned children who do not respect their neglectful parent.

As an adult, Ivan suggests in conversation with Alyosha that his rebellion against God stems from his neglected childhood. While Ivan expresses outrage against the suffering of children whom he does not know, these are expressions of anger against his father's betrayal. He cannot forgive his father for abandoning him; his brand of atheism arises from personal

16. Dostoevsky, *The Brothers Karamazov*, 4.

17. Ibid., 5.

18. Ibid., 9.

19. Ibid., 10.

20. Ibid.

injustice. Although Ivan couches his atheism in theoretical terms, it has concrete origin in his personal background. Ivan's logic would sound something like this: my own suffering is the result of a negligent father; if God is father of all, then the suffering of all is the result of a negligent God. For him, "God the father" induces a negative image, and his parricidal desire corresponds with his spiritual rebellion.

While the plot centers on the three legitimate Karamazov sons, ultimately none of them take their father's life; rather their half-brother Smerdyakov murders Fyodor. Girard divides the guilt among all the brothers, but particularly blames Ivan: "The four brothers are accomplices in the murder of their father, but the guiltiest of all is Ivan, for he is the one who inspires the act of murder. The bastard Smerdyakov is the double of Ivan, whom he admires and hates passionately."[21] Because Ivan's theories motivate Smerdyakov, he is Ivan's double. In front of Grigory, Fyodor, Alyosha, and Ivan, Smerdyakov justifies his intention to apostacize if forced. Even Fyodor notices how Smerdyakov seeks Ivan's approval; he whispers to Ivan, "He wants you to praise him. Praise him."[22] Smerdyakov rejects his foster father's God, convicted by Ivan's theory that God does not exist. And, after Smerdyakov murders Fyodor, he claims that he only acted in accordance with Ivan's ideas.

More abandoned and neglected than any of the Karamazov sons, Smerdyakov is allegedly Fyodor's bastard son by Stinking Lizaveta, an ill-kempt woman in rags and one of Dostoevsky's "holy fools." Grigory recognizes how Smerdyakov "has come from the devil's son and a holy innocent."[23] He is thus an incongruous mix of good and evil. His parents represent two oppositional models. Unfortunately, his holy mother has died, which leaves him with only Fyodor as an exemplar. Neal Bruss ties Smerdyakov's fate to Oedipus: "Fyodor Karamazov provides no model which a son might use to temper his desire and identify himself as a fulfillment and extension of his parents. . . . Fyodor is an extension, or mutation, of previous literary Oedipal villains."[24] If Smerdyakov models Fyodor, he will become an extension of his blasphemous father.

Because Fyodor denies paternity, Smerdyakov feels a more intense rivalry with him than perhaps even his brothers do. Fyodor's rejection has

---

21. Girard, *Resurrection*, 131.

22. Dostoevsky, *The Brothers Karamazov*, 117.

23 Ibid., 89.

24. In addition to Oedipus himself, Bruss ("The Sons Karamazov") mentions Hamlet.

elicited Smerdyakov's hatred and perhaps the boy's propensity towards violence. His foster father Grigory considers Smerdyakov's tendencies "demonic." As a child, Smerdyakov "was very fond of hanging cats, and burying them with great ceremony."[25] Though killing the cats may illustrate his depravity, Smerdyakov counters his viciousness with devout funeral services. In burying these animals, he imitates a priest. The two actions exemplify the extreme war within his soul between his destructive and pious nature. As Smerdyakov ages, he becomes contemplative, and the narrator declares that such contemplation might result in a pilgrimage to Jerusalem "for his soul's salvation, or perhaps he will suddenly set fire to his native village, and perhaps do both."[26] The propensity to imitate both God and Satan is heightened in Smerdyakov, forcing him into an unnatural position. Even Grigory calls him a monster and asks, "Are you a human being?"[27] Part demon and part angel, Smerdyakov resembles Shakespeare's Caliban or Frankenstein's monster. After reading *Paradise Lost*, Frankenstein's monster identifies with Milton's Satan because he conceives of himself as un-fathered. Similarly, rejected by his father and thus conceiving of himself without a father, Smerdyakov devolves into satanic imitation.

When Smerdyakov first speaks as an adult, he publicly renounces the faith of his foster father and amuses his biological father with his carefully reasoned dismissal of divine mystery. At dinner one evening, Grigory recounts the martyrdom of a Russian soldier who did not renounce Christianity and was subsequently "tortured, flayed alive, and died, praising and glorifying Christ."[28] Fyodor mocks such a story, advising that monks should hang up the soldier's skin to draw in paying visitors. After Fyodor's scoffing, Smerdyakov grins in appreciation of his father's cynicism. Smerdyakov reasons that only a couple of ascetic monks in the world have the faith to move mountains, so surely God would not blame those who try to move mountains but cannot and thus succumb to doubt. In his over-rationalized approach to understanding suffering and faith, Smerdyakov mirrors Ivan. However, what is a question of life and death for Ivan is a game for Smerdyakov.

25. Dostoevsky, *The Brothers Karamazov*, 112.
26. Ibid., 115.
27. Ibid., 112.
28. Ibid., 115.

When confronted with reality, both Ivan's and Smerdyakov's rationalizations are undone. Bruss reveals how their arguments turn against themselves:

> [I]f there is no God—that is, if there is no consciousness of the father—then everything is permitted, including parricide. But if there is no father, there can be no parricide. And if there has been parricide—if someone has acted as if everything is permitted—then there had to be a real father, and everything may not be permitted.[29]

With this mind-boggling logical game terrorizing them, Smerdyakov and Ivan suffer inner turmoil in the face of Fyodor's death. Smerdyakov begins reading the sermons of Isaac the Syrian, revealing a potential return to his adopted father Grigory's faith. However, such a possibility seems short-lived for he subsequently hangs himself, proving literal Girard's maxim that "parricide is simultaneously murder and suicide."[30]

Through the rest of the novel Ivan is haunted by unflattering representations of himself, doubles and parodies, including Smerdyakov. In his final interview with Ivan, Smerdyakov repeatedly condemns Ivan for the murder and reduces his own role to that of a mere instrument in Ivan's hand. He insists, "[You] are still responsible for it all. . . . [Y]ou are the only real murderer in the whole affair, and sir, and I am not the real murderer, though I did kill him. You are the rightful murderer."[31] Smerdyakov blames Ivan for theoretically modeling what he carried out. Although Ivan fights to absolve himself—and does so legally—he cannot escape spiritual culpability. Albert Camus summarizes his dilemma thus: "The man who could not understand how one could love one's neighbor cannot understand either how one can kill him."[32] Troubled to discover what his ideas mean in practice, Ivan sinks into madness.

The parricide occurs because Smerdyakov follows Ivan's moral theory, and in the courtroom, the attorney Fetyukovich justifies such a murder according to the same standards. Fetyukovich parodies Ivan's ideas, using them as rhetorical manipulation of his audience. The defense attorney mimics Ivan's "rationalism and an appeal to a sentimental humanitarianism, deriving from Christian principles," though he abuses these Christian

29. Bruss, "The Sons Karamazov," 55.

30. Girard, *Resurrection*, 57.

31. Dostoevsky, *The Brothers Karamazov*, 594.

32. Camus, *The Rebel*, 59.

principles.[33] Fetyukovich separates compassion from Christ, in the same manner that Ivan has: "[I]f we want to be humane—Christian, in fact—we must, and ought to, act only upon convictions justified by reason and experience, which have been passed through the crucible of analysis."[34] All human motivation is reduced to what is reasonable, and Scriptures are manipulated to support humans' rational arguments. To indict Fyodor, and by implication to exonerate Dmitry, Fetyukovich quotes Paul's injunction for fathers not to exasperate their children, distorting the New Testament for his own ends.[35]

Furthermore, Fetyukovich redefines "father" and "parricide" to justify Dmitry's actions. Fetyukovich attempts to pull down heavenly truth to the earthly plane to be evaluated. A father must be worthy of the word; he must be able to answer his child's question, "Why should I love you?"[36] Ivan asks Fetyukovich's question of God, and "in the absence of a rationally satisfactory answer he turns his back on God, just as he also turns his back on his earthly father."[37] When Ivan questions God about the tortured children, he refuses to hear God's answer. Instead, he believes in a silent Christ. Similarly, Ivan deems his father incapable of answering his protests against him, so he rejects him as well.

Fetyukovich assumes that this parricidal desire will register with his audience, and though he speaks on behalf of reason, he plays mostly to their emotions. As though knowing the power of mimesis, the defense attorney puts forth poetry—similar to the form of Ivan's "The Legend of the Grand Inquisitor"—as a way to seduce the mass audience to sympathize with his client. The ploy works in so far as the audience bursts into rapture: "women wept, many of the men also wept, even two of the dignitaries shed tears."[38] One thinks of Dante's Francesca misquoting Augustine to move Dante to faint at her fate. The attorney has produced an emotional storm among his hearers, however, they do not choose to act upon this reaction. The prosecutor's final speech sees through the lies of the defense attorney's rhetoric and shows it to be the worst kind of "novel" with Smerdyakov placed as "some sort of Byronic hero revenging himself upon society for his ille-

33. Dostoevsky, *The Brothers Karamazov*, 697.
34. Ibid., 708.
35. Ephesians 6:4 (NIV); Colossians 3:21 (NIV).
36. Dostoevsky, *The Brothers Karamazov*, 708.
37. Leatherbarrow, *Dostoevsky*, 35.
38. Dostoevsky, *The Brothers Karamazov*, 748.

gitimate birth."[39] Ultimately, in the conclusion of *The Brothers Karamazov*, Dostoevsky gives the victory to the jury that affirms that whether or not Fyodor merited fatherhood, he did not deserve to be murdered.

In his correspondence with an unidentified mother (March 27, 1878), Dostoevsky relates Fetyukovich's question to her, cautioning her that if her child asks whether she deserves love, there is no correct answer. So, Dostoevsky advises, "You must ensure that *he never comes to you* with such a question. And this will only be possible if he loves you directly and spontaneously, so that there is no way the question can enter his head."[40] For Dostoevsky, this question only arises when parents mistreat their children. Several biographies portray Dostoevsky's father as a monster who mistreated his son. Even if he was not this monster, according to Frank, he was "a stern, harsh, exactingly censorious task-master, quite unforgiving of any human weakness and error."[41] Though Mikhail Andreevich Dostoevsky encouraged his children's education and moral development, his figure looms ominously over Dostoevsky. Whether or not Dostoevsky suffered parricidal impulses toward his father, as Freud suggests, he did question whether his father deserved his love.

In contrast to his own upbringing, Dostoevsky doted on his children. Each evening he dined with them, told them fairy tales, and blessed them before bed with the Lord's Prayer. On his death bed, Dostoevsky requested that "the parable of the Prodigal Son be read to the children," and he advised them "to trust God as their Father, plead with Him for forgiveness, and be certain that He would rejoice in their repentance, just as the father had done on the return of the Prodigal Son."[42] This master novelist imitated Scripture in his life, passing down good models for his children. Even Dostoevsky's final words are from a father to his children in imitation of the Father and of the Son.

FROM PARRICIDE TO SUICIDE, HOMICIDE, AND DEICIDE IN *WISE BLOOD*

When Dostoevsky died, he reminded his children that their father would always love them, embracing his children even beyond death. When

39. Ibid.
40. Quoted in Leatherbarrow, *The Brothers Karamazov*, 15.
41. Frank, *Dostoevsky: The Mantle of the Prophet*, 247.
42. Ibid., 748.

O'Connor was only a teenager, her father Edward died of lupus. Her biographer Brad Gooch observes that the surplus of widows and orphans in her fiction "implies a missing husband and father. O'Connor's two novels, and many of her stories, are filled with the eraser marks of all these dead fathers."[43] Because their absence is not volitional, the missing fathers in O'Connor's fiction do not suggest neglect. O'Connor does not connect her deceased father with an absent God, but the absentee fathers in her stories do represent the lack of any valid authority. Thus, the fatherless world of her fiction resembles a godless one.

Often characters reflect on their missing fathers with satisfaction, as though freed from an undesirable burden. In the "Enduring Chill," Asbury loses his father at a young age, an event he considers "a great blessing. . . . [H]e knew he would not have been able to stomach him. He had read some of his correspondence and had been appalled by its stupidity."[44] Asbury reflects the same pride and antagonism towards his mother as well. In "The Comforts of Home" Thomas has inherited such resentment towards his mother from his father. Though "he had not been able to endure [his father] in life," Thomas knows "[the] old man would have had none of this foolishness [of Thomas's mother]."[45] In imitation of his father, Thomas attempts to force his will upon his mother, even though his role in the family may be one of submission to his mother's authority. Thomas deceives himself that he "inherited his father's reason without his ruthlessness and his mother's love of good without her tendency to pursue it."[46] In reality, Thomas has inherited his father's ruthlessness, but without his mother's active love. As though acting out his subliminal desire, Thomas unintentionally shoots his mother at the conclusion of the story.

Like those who read Dostoevsky's biography into his novel, critics occasionally misconstrue O'Connor's work as biographical, specifically when in examining the mother-daughter relationships. Less than five years after O'Connor's death, Josephine Hendin, visited Regina Cline O'Connor in Milledgeville. She portrays Regina as a stifling influence that caged O'Connor in a monotonous farm life and a charade of Southern gentility:

> The fiction O'Connor lived had its roots in that Southern need to
> do pretty regardless of what you feel, and in her own remarkable

43. Gooch, *Flannery*, 71.
44. O'Connor, *Collected Works*, 554.
45. Ibid., 577.
46. Ibid.

ability to divorce behavior from feeling and even to conceal feelings from herself.[47]

For the greatness of O'Connor's fiction, Hendin credits a supposed, suppressed rage in O'Connor against her surroundings and most specifically, against her mother.

When Hendin analyzes O'Connor's stories, she determines to unearth evidence against Regina for crippling O'Connor. She writes: "[O'Connor] often presents her mothers from the point of view of a helpless child to whom they seem superhuman and omnipotent."[48] These passive children include Asbury Fox, Thomas, and Julian, sons who actively hurt or even kill their mothers. Hendin saw the actions of these children as O'Connor's way of acting out against her mother, rebelling through her fiction. According to Hendin,

> [W]hat emerges most powerfully from her work is not the moral that it is wrong to want to destroy your parents. What explodes from these stories is the sheer agony of confronting a mother whose insensitivity renders you furious and whose politeness makes you impotent.[49]

In addition to lacking any sensitivity, Hendin's analysis lacks sufficient evidence. She conjectures that O'Connor acts out a resentment that even she was unaware of.

Brad Gooch offers a more balanced reading of O'Connor's mother. He softens the harsh depictions:

> Regina was both a godsend and a challenge for the daughter she persisted in calling 'Mary Flannery.' Having matured from a comely Southern belle into a feisty, formidable widow, with a straight back, sharp nose, small chin, and enormous black eyes, she countered Flannery's near silence with endless garrulousness, and a zest for money making. . . . She was also an ideal nurse and caretaker, but, at times, as trying a companion for Flannery as she had been for Edward [her husband].[50]

That Regina may have been a taxing presence does not mean that she was not also a blessing. Gooch proposes that Regina needed to manage the

47. Hendin, *The World of Flannery O'Connor*, 13.
48. Ibid., 99.
49. Ibid.
50. Gooch, *Flannery*, 197.

farm and to pinch pennies in order to provide properly for O'Connor in her declining health. Though Gooch describes Regina as a petite villain in appearance, he recognizes the goodness in her domineering tendencies, quoting one of O'Connor's friends: "Regina was a tyrant—though a beloved one."[51] In any case, Regina should not be conflated with the mother characters in O'Connor's stories any more than the tyrannical figure of Fyodor should be read as Mikhail Dostoevsky.

Rather, the characters in O'Connor's stories are the next generation, surrogate children of Ivan Karamazov, whose parricidal desire has bred more spiritual familicide as well as physical violence, so that brothers attack each other, parents disown their children, and grandfathers kill their grandchildren.[52] In many of O'Connor's stories, the children blatantly disregard the parents, disrespecting what they deem supercilious faith or outdated reliance on manners and decorum. O'Connor's stories are peppered with these inconsistent parents and "free-thinking" children. Ralph Wood connects O'Connor's emphasis on familial relationship to Dostoevsky:

> O'Connor may have come to understand the theological quality of the parent-child relationship through her reading of Dostoevsky. For him, it is the primal relationship: our regard for our parents is the most fundamental index of our moral and religious character.[53]

The children's disregard for their parents and arrogant insistence on being self-begotten, autonomous agents is inherited from the Karamazovs. Rather than physical parricide, most commonly these children participate in spiritual parricide, their hate for their parents stewing inside of them. However, when this hate rises to the surface, it results in violence, even in murder.

There is a litany of examples in O'Connor's fiction of these ungrateful offspring, including Asbury, Thomas, and Julian, as well as Scofield and

51. Ibid.

52. In addition to being spiritual more than physical, the parricide in O'Connor's fiction is often directed more towards the mothers than the fathers. Perhaps this difference is rooted in the biographies of the authors—Dostoevsky struggled with his father while O'Connor lost her father at a young age and was raised by her mother. The struggles between father and son, fathers and daughters, mothers and sons, and mothers and daughters differ in more ways than the scope of this project can explore. For a stronger examination of the father-daughter relationship in Southern fiction, see Patricia Yaeger and Beth Kowaleski-Wallace, eds., *Refiguring the Father*.

53. Wood, *Christ-Haunted South*, 211.

Wesley May. Unlike Ivan, who hates his father for his lack of goodness, these children despise their parents for their ignorance or simple values. This progeny is arrogant and proud, vices well exemplified by Mrs. May's sons. They laugh at their mother, condescendingly calling her "Sweetheart" and "Sugarpie," sentimental terms of false endearment. She constantly threatens them with her approaching death, anxious about what her children will do with her property, the legacy of her hard work. Her son Wesley coldly informs her, "I wouldn't milk a cow to save your soul from hell."[54] The verb used by the narrator to describe the sons' actions is usually "hate," much of which centers on their family. Denying their mother's authority, denying even her maternity, Wesley says to his brother, "[N]either you nor me is her boy."[55] Out of arrogance, these sons reject their mother and by refusing to help her, inadvertently aid in her death.

"Everything that Rises Must Converge" shows a more direct link between a child's pride and his parent's death. Though neither Julian nor his mother is without fault in the story, he exhibits a vicious parricidal desire that concludes in his mother's mental degeneration. As with many of O'Connor's main characters, Julian has a false sense of his own importance based on blindness to his own limitations. The mother has shown active love towards Julian by sacrificing her own needs for his needs, yet he refuses to accept such love. In return for her sacrifices, he attempts "to break her spirit," to make himself a so-called "martyr" to her repression, and ironically, "to teach her a lesson" about her self-righteousness.[56]

Like other characters previously mentioned, Julian misconstrues the relationships between love and reason, self and other, freedom and authority. He thinks to himself, "Most miraculous of all, instead of being blinded by love for her as she was for him, he had cut himself emotionally free of her and could see her with complete objectivity. He was not dominated by his mother."[57] Julian favors his ability to rationally and objectively judge his mother over her ability to love him without judgment. He misunderstands that whereas her love allows her to view him as a person, his emotional distance reduces her to an object. Moreover, he frees himself from what he considers her domination, which has consisted of her selflessly sacrificing

54. O'Connor, *Collected Works*, 510.
55. Ibid., 517.
56. Ibid., 489, 486, 493.
57. Ibid., 492.

for him. More than Julian's intellectual pride, his self-importance has caused him to spurn his mother.

Julian has inverted their roles and subsumed his mother's authority. He treats her as though she is the child and he is the parent, but for him, this relationship includes debasing rather than serving the other. When his mother offends a "Negro woman" by offering a penny to the woman's son, the woman knocks her down. Julian responds with hatred: "You got exactly what you deserved."[58] He acts as though he taught his mother this lesson, as though he triumphed in her fall. He admonishes her for her foolishness: "I hate to see you behave like this. . . . Just like a child. I should expect more of you."[59] Then he looks into her face, and he receives his "lesson," for staring back at him is "a face he had never seen before."[60] His mother has suffered a stroke. Only after Julian witnesses her affliction does he recognize his guilt: "The tide of darkness seemed to sweep him back to her, postponing from moment to moment his entry into the world of guilt and sorrow."[61] The story ends with the adult child reproached indirectly by his dying parent.

From the children to their parents, characters must face themselves in O'Connor's mirror and see the devil's face or the good under construction, but either way, they will see a less than perfect image than the one they present.[62] The denial is one of original sin, which Girard notes, "is no longer the truth about all men as in a religious universe but rather each individual's secret."[63] While a defense may be made for some of these good-intentioned parents or grandparents, O'Connor does not allow any character to walk away blameless from a story. When the grandmother in "A Good Man is Hard to Find" reaches out to The Misfit and says, "Why you're one of my babies! You're one of my own children!" she acknowledges her responsibility for his rottenness. As I tell my students, who find very little worthwhile in the grandmother's family, such a statement is not a compliment. The grandmother's son and grandchildren are as horrible at heart as The Mis-

58. Ibid., 499.

59. Ibid.

60. Ibid.

61. Ibid.

62. In "The Introduction to a *Memoir of Mary Ann*," O'Connor writes, "Most of us have learned to be dispassionate about evil, to look it in the face and find, as often as not, our own grinning reflections with which we do not argue, but good is another matter. Few have stared at that long enough to accept that its face too is grotesque, that in us the good is something under construction" (*Mystery and Manners*, 226).

63. Girard, *Deceit, Desire, and the Novel*, 57.

fit is behaviorally. Yet, in this moment, she recognizes a shared flaw, what Western thought once assumed for centuries was a truth about humankind, and what Father Zosima calls our responsibility for all and to all.

Without wanting to acknowledge their sinful nature, many of the parents and grandparents in O'Connor's stories have trouble facing their responsibility for the viciousness of their offspring. They do not realize that their poor modeling has increased the wickedness of their children. For instance, in "The Artificial Nigger," Mr. Head knows that the physical resemblance between him and his grandson is strong but refuses to see any spiritual correlation. The narrator comments, "They were grandfather and grandson but they looked enough alike to be brothers."[64] O'Connor draws these physical mirrors to emphasize the mimetic rivalry between the family members; she does so in numerous other places—between Mr. Fortune and his granddaughter, between Hazel Motes and his grandfather, or between Rayber and Tarwater. Although Mr. Head contrives to counteract his grandson Nelson's pride, he misses how much he himself needs such a tutorial.

After wandering aimlessly in the city, Mr. Head abandons Nelson, leaving him to navigate the streets according to his own ability. In this way, Mr. Head hopes to prove that Nelson should submit to his direction. When the boy rushes down the streets in fear, he accidentally causes a woman to trip. Mr. Head reappears on the scene, but when the woman screams at Mr. Head, he denies any relationship to Nelson: "This is not my boy. . . . I never seen him before."[65] His language recalls Wesley's denial of Mrs. May—that neither him nor Scofield were her boys. The crowd that has gathered around the trio begins to drop back, "staring at [Mr. Head] with horror, as if they were so repulsed by a man who would deny his own image and likeness."[66] In the same way that Mr. Head has blindly refused to see his reflection in Nelson, he now publicly denies culpability.

Only after committing this grievous sin against his grandson does Mr. Head realize his responsibility. He worries that "his sins would be visited upon Nelson and that even now, he was leading the boy to his doom."[67] Mr. Head recognizes that he is Nelson's model, not his rival, and how

---

64. O'Connor, *Collected Works*, 212.

65. Ibid., 226.

66. Ibid.

67. Ibid., 227.

problematic his fight for autonomy has been. John Sykes indicates that this story exemplifies a similar authority conflict found in Dostoevsky:

> Mr. Head and Nelson, in their constant and often comic battle of wills, actually carry out the ancient and universal attempt to supplant God. Their will to power, by a turn Nietzsche and Dostoevsky would have appreciated, informs even their morality.[68]

Sykes's allusion to Dostoevsky seems to conflate the author with the Karamazovs. Yet Sykes accurately characterizes Mr. Head's rejection of Nelson as godless. For in prizing his autonomy more than his responsibility, Mr. Head disregards God's authority.

In the godless world that O'Connor showcases, the myth of autonomy has been embraced by her characters. Girard reflects that such a lie has been the inclination of "every 'new' Western doctrine: God is dead, man must take his place."[69] The parents and grandparents in these stories assert their desire that the children think for themselves. Yet, in practice, they want these children—who physically reflect them—to conform to their image, to think like them. As a child, Whittaker Chambers recalls this inconsistency in his mother's teaching. He recounts a moment when she was trimming the crust off of a pie, as he rambled about "when God made the world." This innocuous phrase causes his non-religious mother to pause her pie-making and scold him: "You must learn to think for yourself. You must keep an open mind and not accept other people's opinions. The world was formed by gases cooling in space."[70] While his mother chastises Chambers for his belief in God and advises him to think for himself, she ultimately pushes him to adopt her beliefs. He writes:

> What impressed me was that [her statement] was an opinion, too, since other people believed something else. Then, why had my mother told me what to think? Clearly, if the open mind was open ... truth was simply a question of which opening you preferred. In effect, the open mind was always closed at one end.[71]

Chambers's anecdote would make great fodder for an O'Connor story; it already possesses a prime ingredient—the parent who ironically exposes her inconsistency before her child. His mother's contradiction represents a

---

68. Sykes, *Aesthetic of Revelation*, 57.
69. Girard, *Deceit, Desire and the Novel*, 57.
70. Chambers, *Witness*, 116–17.
71. Ibid., 117.

modern conundrum for parents: they want their children to reject all previous authority, primarily God's authority, yet they want obedient children who agree with their parents' conclusions about the world. When Chambers's mother instructed him to think for himself, she did not expect that such thoughts would renounce her own.

However, if children are encouraged to reject authority and live autonomously, they will reject even their parents or grandparents' authority, a truth Mr. Fortune learns in "A View of the Woods." Unlike O'Connor's usual old men, Mr. Fortune represents the voice of modern progress. When his daughter's family moves onto a piece of his property, he adopts one of the children as his own. Mary Fortune "looked like her grandfather" and "was like him on the inside too. She had, to a singular degree, his intelligence, strong will, and his push and drive."[72] Because of their similarities, the grandfather adopts Mary Fortune and makes her sole beneficiary of his will. Mr. Fortune encourages Mary's rejection of authority, except when it rebuffs him. For instance, early in the story, the little girl walks dangerously near an embankment, but the grandfather's caution goes unheeded. Though he tries, she ignores him: "She had a habit of his of not hearing what she didn't want to hear and since this was a little trick he had taught her himself, he had to admire the way she practiced it."[73] She imitates his poor behavior, of which he approves until it turns against him.

Though named for him and the beneficiary of his will, Mary Fortune remains loyal to her family, a piety denied by Mr. Fortune. When Mr. Fortune decides to sell the land where Mary's father, Mr. Pitts, grazes his cattle, Mary's family is threatened. Duty-bound to her biological father, Mary Fortune Pitts grows increasingly angry towards her grandfather, who has always acted as a father toward her. When he exclaims, "Are you a Fortune . . . or are you a Pitts? Make up your mind," she retorts, "I'm Mary—Fortune—Pitts," claiming both names.[74] The rivalry intensifies after Mr. Fortune sells the property and threatens to whip her. He has created a hellion, who, in accordance with his teachings, will not submit. She flies at him, biting, flailing, and kicking: "The old man looked up into his own image. It was triumphant and hostile."[75] Mr. Fortune recognizes his own rebellion turning against him, and he will not be overcome. Though

72. O'Connor, *Collected Works*, 525–26.

73. Ibid., 529.

74. Ibid., 541.

75. Ibid., 545.

he has taught her autonomy, it has instigated her parricidal desire, which Mr. Fortune subsequently overcomes with greater violence. Grabbing his granddaughter by the throat, he beats her head into a rock and then stares "at his conquered image."[76] Yet the grandfather has conquered nothing, for by murdering his granddaughter, he has destroyed his progeny. "A View of the Woods" illustrates that prolicide and suicide may be intimately connected. Progeny stem from the self and reflect that self in another, so that to kill one's descendants is to kill part of the self. Moreover, parricide connects with suicide because to kill the source of one's self is to annihilate the self.

The problem for the characters in O'Connor's stories is that the parents and children serve to remind each other that no one is absolutely autonomous. Mothers such as Julian's prompt their children to recognize that they are not self-begotten creatures, that they have an origin apart from themselves. For similar reasons do people reject God—he reminds them of their origin and asks them to renounce their self for the good of others. O'Connor reveals autonomy as the identifying feature of many of her characters, so any relationships that disrupt this autonomy are intolerable.

"THE CHURCH WITHOUT CHRIST" AS "CARICATURAL ULTRA-CHRISTIANITY"

The quest for the autonomous self has dominated the religious landscape in America since before O'Connor's time and up until now. Her fiction yells prophetically forward about the disintegration of the church into an "Elks Club,"[77] in which the divinity of the body of Christ has been removed. In her vision, when Christ is removed, when the "Church without Christ" is preached, the prophets and followers of this belief system are, in actuality, proselytizing the church of the self. Her first novel *Wise Blood* illustrates this problem: the protagonist Hazel Motes attempts to blaspheme Jesus, establishing his new "Protestant" church, only to discover that he cannot shock his audience because they are already heretics, comfortable in their own versions of the Church without Christ.

Hazel Motes has come to the city of Taulkinham to scandalize those around him with his apostasy. On the train ride, he attempts to shock

76. Ibid.

77. This quote is from a letter (June 21, 1959) in defense of the church as the body of Christ: "If the church is not a divine institution, it will turn into an Elks Club" (O'Connor, *The Habit of Being*, 337).

the woman sitting across from him by asking, "Do you think I believe in Jesus?"[78] Before she can answer, he responds, "Well I wouldn't even if He existed. Even if He was on this train."[79] Like the Grand Inquisitor who denied Jesus to his face, Hazel is determined to denounce the Christian God. However, unlike the perturbed Alyosha, Haze's heresy does not shake the woman because, as Hazel comes to realize by the end of the novel, everyone around him is more of an atheist than he is. In fact, it seems people stopped believing in God a long time ago. Thus, when Hazel wakes in a night terror on the train and cries out, "Jesus," the porter responds, "Jesus been a long time gone."[80] Haze slowly realizes that he has returned from the war to preach not good news or bad news but old news.

Since Haze was twelve years old, he has assumed he would become a preacher like his grandfather. The old man "had traveled three counties in a Ford automobile. . . . He would climb up on the nose of it and preach from there and sometimes he would climb onto the top of it and shout down at them."[81] Hazel recalls him preaching about Jesus' death for everyone's souls, including Haze's. His grandfather would point him out in the crowd, though O'Connor parenthetically notes the mimetic rivalry between the two: "The old man . . . had a particular disrespect for [Haze] because his own face was repeated almost exactly in the child's and seemed to mock him."[82] For those who read O'Connor's short stories, the characters of Mr. Fortune and Mr. Head are imbedded in this portrayal. The grandfather becomes an ironic model for Hazel who does mock his ancestor by later standing atop a car and preaching an opposing message. Moreover, the old man's distaste for Haze's mirror image foreshadows Hazel's hostility towards Solace Layfield. These images of the self as human or as mockable discomfit those who profess themselves to be as gods.

In opposition to his grandfather, Hazel's father is a buffoonish atheist reminiscent of Fyodor Karamazov. His father is also called "the old man" in Haze's recollections; he remembers him humped over on his hands and knees in his coffin in a vain attempt not to be buried: "'If I keep my can in

---

78. When O'Connor refers to Jesus, she uses capital letters, even when characters seem blasphemous. However, when Hazel preaches the "new jesus," she keeps the lower case, emphasizing that he does not refer to the actual Jesus here. The change in capitalization underscores the juxtaposition of reality and Hazel's professions.

79. O'Connor, *Collected Works*, 7.

80. Ibid., 4.

81. Ibid., 10.

82. Ibid., 11.

the air,' he heard the old man say, 'nobody can shut nothing on me.'"[83] The two pose competing models for Hazel: on the one hand is his grandfather preaching about the death of Jesus to redeem souls, while on the other is his father's absurdly posed dead body in a coffin. Although Hazel rejects both, he thus imitates both unwillingly. First, he claims a "strong confidence in his power to resist evil; it was something he had inherited, like his face, from his grandfather."[84] Yet, this inheritance has blinded him to his need for redemption and recognition of his own mortality.

These memories of his father and grandfather began with the image of his grandfather in a coffin, followed by his dead younger brothers, and his father's burial. Tallying these physical deaths as a prologue to his grandfather's preaching on Jesus' sacrifice and resurrection, Hazel subconsciously weighs the deaths as evidence against the validity of his grandfather's claims. He experiences a "deep black wordless conviction in him that the way to avoid Jesus was to avoid sin."[85] Not only does Hazel wish to avoid his father's and his grandfather's models, but he even desires to avoid Jesus' model. After this list of dead models, the first chapter concludes with a vision of Hazel's mother's burial. Here, the guarantee of death prevails over Jesus' promise of resurrection.

When Hazel founds his blasphemous church, he follows an American tradition. The "Church without Christ" is the American religion, one that Harold Bloom proves is Gnostic at its core.[86] O'Connor jumps back a century for the source of Gnosticism to an American philosopher, Ralph Waldo Emerson. She writes, "When Emerson decided, in 1832, that he could no longer celebrate the Lord's Supper unless the bread and wine were removed, an important step in the vaporization of religion in America was taken, and the spirit of that step has continued apace."[87] Emerson is a Gnostic or a Cartesian in that he divides and conflates spirit and nature, confusing the two as often as removing one from the other. For him, the physical elements were unnecessary because the spirit dines on spiritual things.

In concurrence with O'Connor, author of *Bad Religion* Ross Douthat calls Emerson the "originator of the American-style God Within theology."

---

83. Ibid., 10.

84. Ibid., 11.

85. Ibid.

86. In *The American Religion*, Bloom argues that American religion is all Gnosticism.

87. O'Connor, *Mystery and Manners*, 161. In *American Nietzsche*, Jennifer Ratner-Rosenhagen shows Emerson's influence on Nietzsche's denouncement of Christianity.

Douthat notes that the real "Jesus of Nazareth" is also inconsequential to this version of Christianity. He cites Emerson's misquotation of Jesus' words: "I am divine. Through me, God acts; through me, speaks. Would you see God, see me, or see thee, when thou also thinkest as I think."[88] Because Emerson confers divinity on each person indiscriminately, the actual incarnation is irrelevant, which, of course, marks it as unauthoritative and improbable. In American Christianity, the self is god.

In this version of the church, the powerless Christ from Ivan Karamazov's poem has been removed all together, even as a façade. To any passerby who will listen, Hazel sermonizes:

> I preach the Church Without Christ. I'm member and preacher to that church where the blind don't see and the lame don't walk and what's dead stay that ways. Ask me about that church and I'll tell you it's the church that the blood of Jesus don't foul with redemption.[89]

Hazel has extracted the supernatural and demythologized the scriptural Jesus, making him a monophysite, just as Ivan did. As Haze tells Sabbath Lily, "I believe in a new kind of Jesus.... [H]e's all man ain't got any God in him."[90] On this foundation, Hazel sets up the Church without Christ.

O'Connor opposes this twentieth-century American version of the Church, defending its divine foundation. She writes (June 21, 1959), "For us [Catholics] the Church is the body of Christ, Christ continuing in time and as such a divine institution. The Protestant considers this idolatry."[91] Hazel has denied the eternity of the church by denying the divinity of Christ. Notably, when Mrs. Flood asks what kind of Church he preaches for, he answers, "Protestant," echoing O'Connor's sentiment that Protestants may consider a divine church idolatrous.[92] Perhaps this is why O'Connor claims, "[N]o one but a Catholic could have written *Wise Blood* even though it is a book about a kind of Protestant saint."[93] O'Connor depicts the rampant belief in this god of the self that has come to replace the Christian God within American churches.

---

88. The quotation is from Emerson's Harvard Divinity School Address, July 15, 1838. Cited in Douthat, *Bad Religion*, 219.

89. O'Connor, *Collected Works*, 59.

90. O'Connor, *Wise Blood*, 121.

91. O'Connor, *The Habit of Being*, 337.

92. O'Connor, *Collected Works*, 60.

93. O'Connor, *The Habit of Being*, 69.

Only a decade after *Wise Blood* was published, the theology of Hazel Motes picks up traction in works such as Gabriel Vahanian's *The Death of God*. In his conclusion, Vahanian offers only two options for those of us living in the post-Christian era—to be gods or wolves to one another. He writes, "[A]lthough [modern atheism] attempts to define man in terms of his relatedness to others, it can only project man as a god or a wolf to his fellow man."[94] In Girard's understanding, the god or the wolf amount to the same thing, a conclusion O'Connor concedes in *Wise Blood*. Not only does Hazel establish himself as a god unto himself and thus act as a wolf towards others, but also the culture that he lives in exemplifies the deified violence that Girard alludes to.

What Vahanian calls "post-Christian," Girard clarifies is actually "caricatural 'ultra-Christianity.'" The debate involves more than semantics and terms, however. For Girard, Americans try "to escape from the Judeo-Christian orbit by 'radicalizing' the concern for victims in an anti-Christian manner."[95] We saw this in Ivan's and Rayber's tenderness for the faceless sufferers. Because Girard contends that the religious impulse is unavoidable, he proves that those who reject God, the death of God theologians or post-Christian secularists, will replaces the Judeo-Christian response to suffering with a faux religious instinct, what he calls "victimology." Girard argues that the "radicalization of contemporary victimology produces . . . a return to all sorts of pagan practices: abortion, euthanasia, sexual undifferentiation, Roman circus games galore but without the victims, etc."[96] Unlike other theories of secularization that view the trends as banal in their vices, Girard draws a link between the loss of Christianity and the increase in forms of violence.

Wise Blood depicts a neo-pagan world, which some critics have seen as absurd, but is American religion magnified, or depicted in caricature, to use Girard's modifier. O'Connor herself described her artistic process as drawing "large and startling figures" to make the repugnancies of modern life "appear as distortions to an audience which is used to seeing them as natural."[97] Sabbath Lily is an example of a neo-pagan amplified. Only bits of her story appear throughout *Wise Blood*, and when pieced together, they create an impression like Picasso's *Les Demoiselles d'Avignon*. A "bas-

---

94. Vahanian, *The Death of God*, 231.

95. Girard, *I See Satan*, 178.

96. Ibid., 181.

97. O'Connor, *Mystery and Manners*, 34.

tard," she travels around with her father who is a disgraced preacher who attempted to blind himself but backed out. According to one of her stories about an unidentified "child"—who may have be understood as Sabbath Lily herself—she was "locked up in a chicken crate" by her grandmother who hung herself with a well rope.[98] Because of her birth as a bastard, Sabbath Lily considers herself damned. Thus, she commits sin blatantly without thought of repercussions.

Although Haze sets out to seduce Sabbath Lily and steal her innocence, she shocks him with her forwardness. As she attempts to entice him into getting "better acquainted," Sabbath Lily relates her correspondence with an advice columnist Mary Brittle. The letters reveal the modern distortions that O'Connor wanted to portray. Brittle advises Sabbath: "Perhaps you ought to re-examine your religious values to see if they meet your needs in Life. A religious experience can be a beautiful addition to living if you put it in the proper perspective and do not let it warf you."[99] Sabbath has memorized this letter and recites it to Haze while trying to coax him into promiscuous sex. The context of the conversation underlines that Sabbath concurs with Brittle's evaluation of religion; it should be satisfying to the self without making demands of the self. The word *value* dismisses any intrinsic merit in religious commandments, and the words *proper perspective* and *warf* relegate religion to Sabbath's own estimation. In other words, Brittle advises Sabbath to play god in her own life.

Girard explains that this neo-pagan worldview "locates happiness in the unlimited satisfaction of desires, which means the suppression of all prohibitions."[100] For Brittle and Sabbath Lily, happiness involves promiscuity and religion as therapy for one's needs. However, Girard regards such theory as potentially violent, and Sabbath Lily provides the evidence. When she introduces herself to Haze, she tells a third-person narrative about a man and woman who killed their child: "They strangled it with a silk stocking and hung it up in the chimney."[101] Sabbath Lily's ostensible confession recalls another of O'Connor's stories, "A Stroke of Good Fortune," ironically titled because the main character Ruby Hill considers her pregnancy anything but good. She treats her condition like a disease: "She was not going

---

98. O'Connor, *Wise Blood*, 122.

99. Ibid., 119.

100. Girard, *I See Satan*, 181.

101. O'Connor, *Wise Blood*, 32.

to have something waiting in her to make her deader."[102] Rather than view the burgeoning life as bringing her life, Ruby dwells on the death of herself, the loss of her autonomy. She places herself in rivalry for life with the unborn child. These instances of infanticide, whether physical or spiritual, illustrate, in part, Girard's conception of neo-paganism.

This is the world in which Hazel preaches, the one to whom O'Connor shouts, where vices and violence are unnoticeable, covered over by therapy, semantics, and moral relativism. Hazel himself is the most blind to the world around him; he cannot recognize the mendacity that he spouts nor understand the reason for his audience's apathy. When Hazel addresses the crowds about his Christless religion, no one listens to him; however, when the same message is preached with different language, suddenly the crowd is all ears. Rather than be appalled by the heresy, the listeners find it familiar, comforting, and priceless.[103]

O'Connor juxtaposes Hazel's sermons with that of Onnie Jay Holy, the stage name of Hoover Shoats, who attempts to profit from Hazel's idea.[104] Onnie Jay is the descendent of Dostoevsky's attorney Fetyukovich who manipulates language to persuade the jury of Dmitry's innocence. Hazel and Onnie Jay are standing before a movie theater, and after the "picture show was over . . . more people were coming up" to hear them speak, as though exchanging one form of entertainment for another.[105] A former radio preacher, Onnie Jay has practiced coating his words with sentimentalism. He exploits those with a weak worldview by using sweet, meaningless words to win over Hazel's crowd: "If you want to get anywhere in religion, you got to keep it sweet."[106] Onnie Jay disconnects words from their meaning in the same way that Hazel has separated Christ's humanity from his divinity:

> You don't have to believe nothing you don't understand and approve of. If you don't understand it, it ain't true, and that's all there is to it. . . . [I]t's based on the Bible. . . . It's based on your own personal interpitation of the Bible, friends. You can sit at home and

102. O'Connor, *Collected Works*, 195.

103. This scene reminds me of Douthat's description of Chopra and Oprah. If someone accused them "of being a heretic," they would just put on a "tolerant smile" and suggest "that perhaps you just haven't opened your mind to a broad enough conception of what Christianity really is" (Douthat, *Bad Religion*, 209).

104. "Onnie Jay Holy" is simply pig latin for Jonnie Holy.

105. O'Connor, *Collected Works*, 84.

106. Ibid., 89.

interpit your own Bible, however you feel in your heart it ought to be interpited. That's right . . . just the way Jesus would have done it.[107]

Superseding Hazel's blasphemy, Onnie Jay carries out its implications. For instance, Hazel attests that Jesus did not accomplish miracles; this interpretation removes pieces of Scripture according to the reader's whims.[108] Onnie Jay promotes this aspect of Hazel's church by appealing to the crowd's desire to live "however [they] feel in [their] heart"—a sentiment similar to Mary Brittle's advice to Sabbathy Lily.[109] The encounter with Onnie Jay reveals that Hazel has not accomplished the apostasy he proposes.

Moreover, Hazel confronts his own mendacious image in the prophet, Solace Layfield, that Onnie Jay hires to replace Haze in his money-making scheme to found a new church. The night after meeting Onnie Jay, Haze parks his Essex again in front of the Odeon Theater and preaches, "In yourself right now is the only place you got . . . Your conscience is a trick . . . . [I]t don't exist though you may think it does, and if you think it does, you had best get it out in the open and hunt it down and kill it."[110] Haze establishes his autonomy even in rivalry to his own conscience; he recognizes a divided self and inspires the audience to violently dispose of the spiritual part. When Onnie Jay's prophet stands before him, Haze sees his own conscience threatening his self-image. In shock, he pauses: "He had never pictured himself that way before."[111] To this illusion which accurately portrays Haze to himself, Haze responds by repeating his earlier sermon, though with new intent: "If you don't hunt it down and kill it, it'll hunt down and kill you."[112] Hazel declares his intention to murder Solace Layfield.

Not only does Solace parody Hazel, but also he represents two models whom Hazel has been rejecting throughout the novel, Jesus and Hazel's grandfather. Since his childhood, Hazel has been hounded by Jesus, who moves "from tree to tree in the back of his mind, a wild ragged figure

107. Ibid., 86–87.

108. Of course, Onnie Jay's brief sermon indicts the Protestant notion of individual interpretation of Scriptures. In the Protestant tradition, each person is separately responsible for his or her soul before God. While Holy Scripture is the supreme guidebook for a person's actions, each person must interpret it as an individual. The 1925 Southern Baptist Convention's "Baptist faith and message" gives evidence of these beliefs.

109. O'Connor, Collected Works, 87.

110. Ibid., 93.

111. Ibid., 94.

112. Ibid., 95.

motioning him to turn around and come off into the dark."[113] Before joining the army, Hazel attempted to avoid Jesus by avoiding sin, however, now he has been embracing sin, which brings him face-to-face with his stalker. Also, throughout the novel, Hazel has denied his vocation to preach like his grandfather did. While everyone assumes he's a preacher, Haze has denied this role. His grandfather preached that Jesus would get Hazel in the end, so Haze has been running from both. When Haze murders Solace, he does so in attempt at symbolic, simultaneous patricide and deicide. In reality, the murder is a death of self, and Haze, seemingly without volition, comes to imitate Christ.

After murdering Solace, Haze unwillingly plays priest to the dying man. Haze bends over Solace to hear his dying words, a confession: "Give my mother a lot of trouble . . . . Never giver no rest. Stole theter car. Never told the truth to my daddy or give Henry what, never. . . ."[114] Aghast that he unintentionally acts as a priest to this young man whom he has killed, Hazel pulls back and demands that the man shut up. Solace's last words are "Jesus hep me."[115] Hazel has spent the last few weeks preaching against the immortality of human beings and the divinity of Christ. He has asserted that each person must redeem him or herself here and now, forgetting the past and disregarding the future. However, Solace reverses the damage that Hazel has been attempting by acknowledging the needs of his soul, his responsibility to his parents and others, and the intercessory power of Christ.

Although Hazel wanted to maintain that human beings were no more than physical matter, which could be easily disposed of, his murder revealed the unseen reality to him. O'Connor writes (Aug. 2, 1955), "I think sin occasionally brings one closer to God."[116] In this case, Hazel experiences a connection between deicide and violence. Hazel sought to live as though God did not exist, and he made himself his own deity. Unfortunately, Hazel's attempt to be godlike leads him to act as a wolf towards others.

Furthermore, all of Hazel's posturing and fighting has only reaffirmed the existence of Christ. While Hazel founds the Church without Christ on deicide, he seems ignorant of the irony that the Church of Christ is also founded on the death of Jesus Christ of Nazareth in the first century. Hazel can only establish his church in opposition to this specific Jesus Christ,

113. Ibid., 11.
114. Ibid., 115.
115. Ibid.
116. O'Connor, *The Habit of Being*, 92.

which concedes more than denies his reality. Just as Alyosha pointed out that Ivan's poem praised Jesus rather than attacked him because it showed "everything in a reverse manner," as Girard notes, "like the negative of a photograph,"[117] so, too, Hazel's intense blasphemy emphasizes the significance of Jesus and his lingering influence. In response to this realization, Hazel carries out violence upon himself. In imitation of Paul who was blinded by God and perhaps of Sabbath Lily's father who attempted but failed to follow through, Haze blinds himself with lime at the end of the novel. Moreover, he carries rocks in his shoes and wires under his shirt, attempting "to pay" for his uncleanliness.[118] Critics debate whether Haze's asceticism here represents a following of Christ or a continuation of his godlike stance towards sanctification. When Asa Hawkes recalls his attempt to blind himself, he notes, "He had been possessed of as many devils as were necessary to do it, but at that instant, they disappeared."[119] Hawkes implies the blinding would have been a demonic action, yet Haze's is often cast as Christian imitation. Mrs. Flood, his landlady, insists, "You must believe in Jesus or you wouldn't do these foolish things."[120] Girard denounces this form of imitation; in his interpretation, Jesus does not "propose an ascetic rule of life in the sense of Thomas a Kempis."[121] He argues that the "desire to sacrifice *oneself* [is to] make *oneself* godlike."[122] Girard warns that sacrificial models potentially sacralize the unsacred. Whether Haze should or not imitate Christ in this form, his actions attempt—for the first time—to follow an authority outside of himself. His death is heavy with symbolism. Resonant of his humble descent, Haze lies in a drainage ditch; moreover, the location is near an abandoned construction project, which recalls O'Connor's language about each person being a good under construction. His last words are, "I want to go on where I'm going."[123] For a man who insisted, "You can't go neither forwards nor backwards," this desire to move on suggests a conversion in his character.[124]

---

117. Girard, *Resurrection*, 66.

118. O'Connor, *Collected Works*, 125.

119. Ibid., 65.

120. Ibid., 127.

121. Girard, *I See Satan*, 13.

122. Girard, *Things Hidden*, 236.

123. O'Connor, *Collected Works*, 131.

124. Ibid., 93.

CONCLUSION

Writing fifty years after O'Connor's death, Douthat sees extended implications of her "Church without Christ." He indicts Oprah, Deepak Chopra, and Elizabeth Gilbert as propagators of this religion in which the self is the highest goal. As the new god, this self must be loved, indulged, and obeyed. However, Douthat alludes to the demonic conclusion of such a belief system: "If pushed too far, the quest for a 'Supreme Self' can blur into the most ancient human temptation, the whisper in Eden that 'ye shall be as gods.'"[125] While American Christians may embrace a faith in which we can think, feel, and act according to whatever Jesus tells us in our hearts, O'Connor worried that this voice may not be of "God within" but of Satan. She writes Bill Sessions (Sept. 29, 1960): "The Catholic believes any voice he may hear comes from the Devil unless it is in accordance with the teaching of the Church."[126] With no other authority but the self, each person's desires can easily fall prey to the demonic, a discomfiting notion, especially in a century predisposed to ignore its reality.

125. Douthat, *Bad Religion,* 230.
126. O'Connor, *The Habit of Being,* 410.

CHAPTER 3

THE DEMONIC AUTHORITY
OF THE AUTONOMOUS SELF

As WITHIN EVERY PERSON so within every literary character of Dostoevsky and O'Connor, the heart is a battleground between the authority of Christ and that of the autonomous self. When Ivan and Rayber, for example, reject God's world, they displace his authority with their own. When a person chooses his or her supposed autonomous self as the authority, she models Satan in his rebellion against God. One of the devil's most deceptive tricks has been to persuade people to stop believing in him,[1] and frequently, he masks himself quite well under the guise of the autonomous self. René Girard writes, "At the heart of everything there is always human pride or God, that is, the two forms of freedom."[2] The former is a false freedom wherein one succumbs to demonic desires; only under God's authority does true freedom exist. Especially in *The Brothers Karamazov* and in *The Violent Bear It Away*, Dostoevsky and O'Connor reveal the satanic imitation of their characters, usually through their interactions with the demonic itself.

---

1. O'Connor makes this assertion: "The devil's greatest wile, Baudelaire has said, is to convince us that he does not exist" (*Mystery and Manners,* 112).

2. Girard, *Resurrection,* 139.

LOSS OF BELIEF IN SATAN

A number of Christian authors of the past two centuries have claimed that the devil erases himself from human awareness primarily by convincing human beings of their own self-sufficiency. In late nineteenth- and early twentieth-century writings, the devil becomes little more than evidence of psychological abnormality, a superstition of the uneducated, or a literary trope. To perpetuate people's delusion, C. S. Lewis's devil Screwtape instructs another demon, Wormwood, to conceal his identity: "Our policy, for the moment, is to conceal ourselves. Of course this has not always been so."[3] The demon explains that they should remain illusory by seducing humans with skeptical materialism. Satan becomes a literary character from the poems of Dante or Milton, but not a supernatural reality.

At some time in the eighteenth century, Satan and all his demonic protégés disappeared from intellectual discourse. In *The Death of Satan*, Andrew Delbanco narrates how Satan vanished from American culture, indicting Enlightenment thinkers who "effected a sweeping reorganization of reality with which we still live: the dispossession of the invisible world as a legitimate object of knowledge."[4] The skeptical materialists that Screwtape and Wormwood desired became the popular naysayers, and they occluded anything supernatural, including Satan. The problem, Delbanco maintains, occurred when the notion of Satan transitioned from an interior to exterior reality, when Satan "turned from an attribute of the self into a visible being outside of the self."[5]

Delbanco charts the dissolution of this belief: while previously associated with the sinful self, the devil becomes an entirely exterior and ultimately comic figure. Lewis's devil advises the lesser demon to perpetuate this image: "If any faint suspicion of your existence begins to arise in [the human's] mind, suggest to him a picture of something in red tights, and persuade him that since he cannot believe in that . . . he therefore cannot believe in you."[6] Lewis depicts the devil as wise concerning the weakness of the modern imagination. Mocked as a red, horned, and odious little beast, the devil vanishes because he does not satisfy the modern desire for empirical proof.

---

3. Lewis, *The Screwtape Letters*, 31.

4. Delbanco, *The Death of Satan*, 73.

5. Ibid., 64.

6. Lewis, *Screwtape*, 32.

Moreover, the rise of individualism inversely relates to belief in the devil as pride, the sin most closely associated with the devil, becomes a virtue. In Judeo-Christian Scriptures, pride is said to come before a fall (Prov 16:18), and it was traditionally acknowledged as the chief of sins. According to the *Oxford English Dictionary*, pride means a "high opinion of oneself" or "a consciousness of what befits [oneself]." Delbanco writes, "Pride of self, once the mark of the devil, was now not just a legitimate emotion but America's uncontested god. And since everyone had his own self, everyone had his own god."[7] Each person imitates Satan's desire to be one's own god, without recognizing any association with the devil.

However, the transition from a culture aware of demonic presences to one that denies them does not necessitate an actual disappearance of the devil. O'Connor affirms her belief in the devil "who is not simply generalized evil, but an evil intelligence determined on its own supremacy."[8] No longer recognizable, the devil continues to deceive people who have no way of identifying the nature of their encounter with evil. Since discarding the reality of the demonic has left culture defenseless against evil, O'Connor asserts the novelist's responsibility to uncloak him:

> [The novelist] may find in the end that instead of reflecting the image at the heart of things, he [or she] has only reflected our broken condition and, through it, the face of the devil we are possessed by. This is a modest achievement, but perhaps a necessary one.[9]

Denis de Rougemont undertakes a task similar to O'Connor's; he offers an exposé of the devil in his monograph *The Devil's Share*, which O'Connor owned in her personal library. Reduced to a caricature, Satan hides within his façade: "Satan dissimulates himself behind his own image."[10] By convincing humans that he does not exist, Satan creates an ever more effective mask. Hence de Rougemont's attempt to expose the real rather than the fabricated adversary.

First, de Rougemont establishes Satan's parasitic nature. Since Satan rebels against the God who calls himself "I AM" in Scripture (Exod 3:14), referring to divine nature as indescribable being, Satan rejects being itself. He rejects existence. De Rougemont writes, "Having refused to serve God,

---

7. Delbanco, *Death of Satan,* 106.

8. O'Connor, *Mystery and Manners,* 168.

9. Ibid., 168.

10. de Rougemont, *The Devil's Share,* 20.

to be of use to God, [Satan] has become the one who serves Nothing, who is of use to Nothing."[11] When Satan attempts to replace being, he loses being, and is thrust from heaven to roam the earth and to feed parasitically off human beings. Satan does not disappear, but his triumphs are limited by the nothingness he serves. As de Rougemont explains, "[Satan's] victories will always be sterile. For one does not become a father by stealing a child. . . . One can steal power, but not authority."[12] While Satan convinces humans to cast off their divine father, his own adoption of them will always be counterfeit; it will always be enslavement posing as freedom.

De Rougemont offers hope to those in rebellion by enabling them to see that divine patronage persists: God remains the father even if Satan enlists God's children. Dostoevsky and O'Connor both give evidence of this truth in their characters' intimations of grace. For instance, Ivan's diatribe against God's injustice in his defense of suffering children is prompted by his unacknowledged awareness of the *imago dei* within each child. In kind, Rayber reveals this divine urge in his early eagerness to hear Mason's Bible stories. Despite the materialistic worldview imposed by his parents, the young Rayber is drawn to Mason's tales of supernatural experiences.

Though rebellion against God does not obviate his presence, the rebel renounces his or her divine freedom to become a slave to autonomous desires, as de Rougemont explains:

> Man *is* free, and this means that he is placed at each moment in a double possibility: that of doing the good which God wishes, which will free him; or that of doing the good he himself wishes according to his desires and by which he immediately finds himself chained. Be free "for nothing," without conditions or aims, be free to do what you please, and you will probably do what pleases the Devil.[13]

In *The Diary of a Writer*, Dostoevsky echoes this paradoxical truth: "License of desires leads only to your enslavement."[14] In concord with the thought of Dostoevsky and O'Connor, de Rougemont indicates that the autonomous will set in opposition to the will of God leads to an unknowing imitation of the demonic.

---

11. Ibid., 30.
12. Ibid., 31.
13. Ibid., 99.
14. Dostoevsky, *The Diary of a Writer*, 623.

Neither Dostoevsky nor O'Connor proposes a dualistic rivalry between God and Satan, but they both acknowledge Satan as a reality manifested by human pride. To defeat Satan, then, is to acknowledge the indestructible divine image planted within every human being, and thus to cry out with the angels, "Who is like God?" De Rougemont asserts that "this cry crushes the Devil, this lance transfixes the serpent who hissed, 'you shall be like gods.'"[15] Because only God is God, all competing gods are his many imposters. Satan is not solitary but Legion: "[W]hile remaining *one* he can assume many diverse aspects as there are individuals in the world."[16] By offering alleged godhood to whoever desires it, Satan manifests himself in many places and persons. The pride that drives characters to replace God's authority with their own subjective moral compass renders them prone to demonic imitation.

GIRARD AND SATANIC IMITATION

Girard defines authority as the model after which a person patterns his or her life and behavior. According to Girard, the key characteristic of human beings is the "mimetic desire," the desire to mimic another. While people assume the "total autonomy of individuals, that is the *autonomy of their desires*," in actuality, they naturally "tend to desire what [their] neighbor has or what [their] neighbor desires."[17] To verify his theory, Girard suggests simply looking at two people who covet the same object. He offers the Decalogue as further evidence. From the perspective of mimesis, the commandments restrain rivalry between people: for instance, the injunctions not to steal from others and not to covet another's wife. For Girard, social rivalry will be decreased or increased by the model a person chooses.

On the moral level, the person chooses whether to model God—absolute being—or Satan—nonbeing. The choice between divine and demonic models is a choice between models who never become obstacles and rivals for their disciples because they desire nothing in a greedy and competitive way [one the one hand,] and [on the other hand] models whose greed for whatever they desire has immediate repercussions on their imitators, transforming them right away into diabolic obstacles.[18] The God who is

15. de Rougemont, *Devil's Share*, 196.
16. Ibid., 44.
17. Girard, *I See Satan*, 8.
18. Ibid., 40.

all desires nothing, while Satan who is nothing desires all. Thus, following the first model leads paradoxically to self-abnegation and fulfillment, while embracing the second model leads to competition and emptiness. Girard notes, "Satan is an imitator in the rivalistic sense of the word. . . . Satan is the ape of God."[19] Rather than truth and life, Satan brings lies and death.

Dostoevsky and O'Connor both believe in an either-or choice between God and Satan as father. In John 8:42–44, Jesus accuses a Jewish crowd of serving Satan as their Father because of their desire to murder him.[20] Jesus says:

> If God were your Father, you would love me, for I proceeded and came forth from God. . . . You are of your father the devil and it is the desires of your father that you wish to do. From the beginning, he was a murderer and had nothing to do with truth because the truth is not in him. When he speaks lies, he draws them from his own nature, because he is a liar and the father of lies.[21]

When Girard references this passage, he underlines Jesus' assertion, "It is the desires of your father that you wish to do." Girard describes this crowd as taking

> the devil as the model for their desires. The desire of which Jesus speaks is therefore based on imitation, whether of the devil or God. . . . To repeat, the idea of the 'father' is here the same thing as the *model* without which human desire, lacking its own proper object, cannot come into being.[22]

Girard makes Jesus' use of the word *father* the conceptual equal of "model." Because the Jewish crowd's desire to murder Jesus models Satan's desire, the crowd's father must be Satan. The choice Jesus sets up, as Girard indicates, is between two models, between two fathers, between God and Satan.[23]

19. Ibid., 45.

20. In her article "Dostoevsky's Markings in the Gospel According to St. John," Irina Kirillova notes Dostoevsky's thick underlining in John, especially of John 8:42–47, where he underlines 8:43 and marks it with an exclamation mark (46).

21. John 8:42–44 (NIV).

22. Girard, *I See Satan*, 40.

23. Let me reiterate my understanding of de Rougemont's notion of fatherhood in conjunction with Girard's notion here because I do not find them contradictory: since God created his children, he remains the parent, and Satan's "fatherhood" will always be false because it is not adoption but enslavement. Humans may choose to follow Satan as their father, but this does not change the reality that God *is* father to everyone. Analogously, a child may deny her biological parents to imitate another adult, but this does not

In the scriptural accounts, Satan's desire to be like God causes his ejection from heaven. The prophet Isaiah refers to Satan as the outcast angel who said in his heart, "I will ascend to heaven; I will raise my throne above the stars of God. . . . I will make myself like the Most High" (Isa 14:13–14). Driven by pride, Satan expresses his desire to replace God in making himself like God. Humans, then, when choosing to follow their own desires are unconsciously mimicking Satan's pride. In Genesis 3:5, Satan tempts Adam and Eve to become "like God." Again, in Matthew 4:9, Satan tempts the Son of God with the desire to be like God and have authority over the world. However, such godlike authority will be granted only if Jesus "will bow down and worship [Satan]," implying that even Christ's authority is conditional on satanic service.

Dostoevsky and O'Connor present this either-or choice as between models. Robert Brinkmeyer notes that in O'Connor's stories, "[e]very person must make a personal choice either to accept Christ into his or her life or to reject him. There is no gray area, no room for compromise: One lives by Christ or the Devil."[24] The third alternative, a life ruled by the self, is simply a disguised form of the latter choice. Dostoevsky agrees. When his former mentor Belinsky dismissed Christ's authority, Dostoevsky replied, "[I]n insulting him, [Belinsky] has never asked himself: 'What are we to put in his place? Ourselves?' No, he has never given a thought to that."[25] When God is displaced from the throne, the autonomous human being assumes authority. Ivan observes something similar, as W. J. Leatherbarrow notes: "[I]f God does not exist or is rejected then 'all is permitted'; human beings are their own masters."[26] According to Dostoevsky and O'Connor, placing the self in the role of God imitates Satan, and thus, the authority of the autonomous self is actually demonic authority.

Dostoevsky and O'Connor expose the freedom of this choice within the heart of each character. In the Author's Note to the second edition of *Wise Blood*, O'Connor writes, "[F]ree will does not mean one will, but many wills conflicting in one man." In keeping both with the Scriptures and the early church fathers, O'Connor understood the heart as a spiritual battleground. Paul in Romans writes, "I do not understand what I do. For what I

---

change who her parents are.

24. Brinkmeyer, *The Art and Vision of Flannery O'Connor*, 33.

25. Letter to Nikolay Nikolayevitch (Dresden, May 18, 1871), in Dostoevsky, *Memoirs, Letters, and Autobiographical Works*.

26. Leatherbarrow, *A Devil's Vaudeville*, 38.

want to do I do not do, but what I hate I do" (Rom 7:15), and his sentiment is echoed by Macarius the Elder, a church father in fourth century Egypt:

> The heart itself is but a small vessel, yet dragons are there, and there are also lions; there are poisonous beasts and all the stockpiles of evil, rough and uneven paths and chasms. But there too is God, the angels, the life and the Kingdom, the light and the apostles, the heavenly cities and the treasures of grace—all things are there.[27]

Dostoevsky and O'Connor both reveal their characters as having hearts filled with these warring demons and angels.

In *Notes from the Underground,* for instance, Dostoevsky displays a human being's divided will. The main character, the Underground Man, narrates his story in the first person, explaining his motivations, confessing his lies, and assessing his own character. He declares how both wickedness and goodness war within him: "I was conscious every moment of so very many elements in myself most opposite to [wickedness]. I felt them simply swarming in me, those opposite elements."[28] Knowing that he should tell the truth, he will purposefully lie and then subsequently condemn himself for such a base deed. Next he will perform a morally upright action—for instance, he shows kindness to a prostitute. Then he will attempt to overturn such goodness by hurting the same woman. This character epitomizes Bakhtinian unfinalizability, reflecting an endless confrontation with the choice between modeling God or Satan.

Anticipating the modern fascination with the divided person, Dostoevsky here creates the first "modern" character, as Steiner writes:

> [T]he assertion that there are within individual men several conflicting personalities, and that baser, ironic, irrational strains of consciousness may be more authentic than the semblance of coherence and reason offered to the outside world, was put forward only in the eighteenth century. It was then, as Berdiaev writes in his study of Dostoevsky, that "a chasm opened in the depths of man himself and therein God and Heaven, the Devil and Hell were revealed anew."[29]

Because of Dostoevsky's dissection of a human personality as containing multiple personalities in conflict, Steiner identifies this underground man

---

27. Macarius, *The Fifty Spiritual Homilies and the Great Letter,* 43.7.

28. Dostoevsky, *Notes from the Underground,* 5.

29. Steiner, *Tolstoy or Dostoevsky,* 218.

as the first "modern" character. Berdiaev correctly diagnoses these multiple divisions as the product of a battle in the human heart between heaven and hell, a notion drawn from the Judeo-Christian tradition. In Dostoevsky's *The Brothers Karamazov*, Dmitry says of the human condition: "Here the devil struggles with God, and the battlefield is the hearts of men."[30] Dmitry accurately depicts the devil as the one struggling against God, for the two are not equally contending forces.

When characters, such as Dmitry, acquiesce to their selfish desires, they lie, steal, and even commit violence against others. Dmitry commits all of the aforementioned acts, considering them small victories of the demon inside him. In answer to the prosecutor's inquiries concerning his crimes, Dmitry continually answers, "The devil knows," a popular Russian idiom. For Girard, Satan "is certainly easier to imitate than Christ . . . for he counsels us to abandon ourselves to all our inclinations in defiance of morality and its prohibitions."[31] In the words of Ivan, "everything is permissible" when Satan is the model. Individual autonomy, or "belief in yourself"[32] to use the popular phrase, has almost come to supplant the ancient Golden Rule, and people easily persuade themselves that they are their own personal gods. However, Girard explains that their status as their own gods is illusory:

> But then suddenly there appears an unexpected obstacle between [people] and the object of [their] desire, and to [their] consternation, just when [they] thought [they] had left Satan far behind [them], it is he, or one of his surrogates, who show up to block the route.[33]

All these personal, individual gods eventually confront each other, and in a battle between false gods, only one may win.

The notion that each person should rule his or her own cosmos sounds appealing, but this seduction quickly degenerates to accusation when the person's will confronts reality. What people have believed to be

---

30. Dostoevsky, *The Brothers Karamazov*, 97.

31. Girard, *I See Satan*, 32.

32. Despite the popularity of this phrase, Dostoevsky and O'Connor might agree more with G. K. Chesterton, who writes in *Orthodoxy* that people who believe in themselves are unconsciously mad: "Complete self-confidence is not merely a sin; complete self-confidence is a weakness. Believing utterly in one's self is a hysterical and superstitious belief . . ." (13).

33. Girard, *I See Satan*, 33.

freedom, they discover is slavery. When their will confronts the unavoidable real—death, for instance—blasphemers realize their diabolic mimicry. Rowan Williams refers to this disjunction between will and reality as the root of demonic:

> [T]he true profaner has elevated his or her reality, chosen isolation from what is commonly known and acknowledged. . . . Only when both the will and the real are fully in play can this sort of thing happen: the essence of the diabolic is, in this connection, that it simply dissolves the real, as Ivan's Devil does with his solipsism and agnosticism.[34]

Though it should not be surprising that the prince of darkness obscures the truth or that the father of lies deceives even his own children, the ploy works because individuals deceive themselves. Girard writes, "Duping oneself is what characterizes the entire satanic process, and that is why one of the titles of the devil . . . is 'prince of darkness.'"[35] For the autonomous self, the will supersedes perception, so a person mimicking Satan will remain blind as long as he or she desires to be.

While individuals choose to remain blind to the demonic nature of their desires, all other people become either rivals to their authority or else pawns to be exploited in achieving their desires. Girard explains:

> The sons of the devil are those who let themselves be taken into the circle of rivalistic desire and who, unknowingly, become the playthings of mimetic violence. Like all the victims of this process, "they do not know what they are doing" (Luke 23:34).[36]

Girard describes those who think they have chosen their own will as acting according to Satan's will more than their own. The word *plaything* is particularly derogatory: ironically, those who choose to be their own god are demoted to mere toys and trinkets. Here, Girard emphasizes the blindness, self-deceit, and ignorance of the sons of the devil, particularly their ignorance of their unacknowledged sonship.

"Rivalistic desire" refers to the inevitable competition between autonomous selves. Girard describes Satan as the fomentor of mimetic contagion. Dostoevsky recognizes that Satan works through this process, though he considers him more as a self-canceling capability within the self.

---

34. Williams, *Language, Faith and Fiction*, 226.

35. Girard, *I See Satan*, 127.

36. Ibid., 40.

Leatherbarrow lists the various references to those characters who live unto themselves in Dostoevsky's novel:

> Zosima's belief that hell is 'the suffering that comes from consciousness that one is no longer able to love' . . . reflects the notion of hell as human solitude. . . . A similar idea—that hell may be the consequence of self-centeredness—lies behind Grushenka's folk tale of the onion and the sinner who tries to save herself at the expense of others, and, rather more obliquely, behind the view of Dmitry's coachman Andrei, on the road to Mokroe, that hell is for those such as grandees, rulers, judges, and rich folk, who ride roughshod over others and "give way to no one."[37]

Each of these characters highlights the connection between self-centeredness and hell: for Dostoevsky, the demonic begins in undefined desire and is fed by selfishness.

Although both Dostoevsky and O'Connor depict devils who are inseparable from the autonomous selfhood of each main character, they differ in their identifications of the devil. In *The Brothers Karamazov* Ivan Karamazov fights the reality of the devil as a separate entity from his self. He accuses the devil, "[Y]our aim is to convince me you exist apart and are not my nightmare."[38] Ivan clings to autonomous reason as if it were an antidote to this manifestation, insisting that the devil is "only one side of me [. . .] of my thoughts and feelings, but only the nastiest and stupidest of them."[39] His dependence on empirical proof, however, prevents him from recognizing the devil's spiritual reality. Ivan misconstrues the devil's existence, yelling: "Never for one minute have I taken you for reality. You are a lie, you are my illness."[40] In truth, the devil inhabits the "stupider" part of Ivan like a spider in a corner of the house, but this does not undermine his reality. Whether or not Dostoevsky credits the devil's objective existence, the lie perpetuated in this scene is the notion that Ivan suffers a mere psychological defect.

In *The Violent Bear It Away*, O'Connor insists on the actual personage of the devil, though he stems from Tarwater's selfishness and delusion. After his great-uncle Mason dies, Tarwater begins "to feel that he was only just now meeting himself, as if as long as his uncle lived, he had been

37. Leatherbarrow, A *Devil's Vaudeville*, 160.
38. Dostoevsky, *The Brothers Karamazov*, 606.
39. Ibid., 603–4.
40. Ibid.

deprived of his own acquaintance."[41] Though not separate from his self, the devil is no less objectively real. O'Connor writes (November 28, 1961): "My Devil has a name, a history and a definite plan. His name is Lucifer, he's a fallen angel, his sin is pride, and his aim is the destruction of the Divine plan."[42] Tarwater's inward "stranger" is a manifestation of this Devil. While O'Connor is more convinced than Dostoevsky about the transcendent reality of the Devil, she presents a character just as hesitant as Ivan to accept this truth. Tarwater's devil feeds him lies: "[T]here ain't no such thing as a devil. I can tell you from my own self-experience. I know that for a fact. It ain't Jesus or the devil. It's Jesus or *you*."[43] By reducing the choice to autonomy versus heteronomy, the devil again accomplishes his masterstroke, convincing Tarwater that the demonic does not exist. As Girard makes clear, this choice masks the actual choice between God and Satan as the models that govern human desire.

DEMONIC PRESENCE IN *THE BROTHERS KARAMAZOV*

The world depicted at the beginning of *The Brothers Karamazov* is one of demonic presence, filled with corruption and rivalry. However, the presence of real devils must be distinguished from that of the caricatured devils that some of the characters describe. For instance, the credulous and superstitious Father Ferapont crushes devils' tails in doors and makes them disappear with signs of the cross. He tells a young monk:

> I saw a devil sitting on one man's chest hiding under his cassock, only his horns poked out; another had one peeping out of his pocket with such sharp eyes, he was afraid of me; another settled in the unclean bellow of one, right in the guts, another was hanging round a man's neck, and he was carrying him about without seeing him.[44]

Ferapont "sees" little devils (*чертей*) crawling all over the monastery like an infestation of insects. Ferapont is thus "seduced by the attraction of 'diabolic' narration," which, as Williams indicates, "is a mark of having *really*

---

41. O'Connor, *Collected Works*, 352.
42. O'Connor, *The Habit of Being*, 456.
43. O'Connor, *Collected Works*, 354.
44. Dostoevsky, *The Brothers Karamazov*, 153.

succumbed to diabolic temptation."[45] Though Fyodor treats devils as jokes while Ferapont takes them seriously, both characters "appeal to the devils of folklore" and thus miss "the genuinely diabolic problem of self-deceit."[46]

As noted earlier, self-deceit is one of the devil's primary tools; it marks the spurious nature of the father of lies. Characters who imitate the devil may be blind to their imitation, but their lies and violence betray their demonic model. For instance, Lise Khokhlakov, whom Ivan calls "that little demon," condemns people for their submission to evil: "[I]t's as though people have made an agreement to lie about it and have lied about it ever since. They all declare that they hate evil, but secretly they love it."[47] Lise reveals that the aptitude for evil and the desire to lie is a form of demonic imitation.

However, Lise vacillates between her desire for salvation and her intense pleasure in trafficking with the demonic. Like Fyodor and Ferapont, she recalls interactions with devils:

> I sometimes dream of devils. It's night, I am in my room with a candle and suddenly there are devils all over the place, in all the corners, under the table, and they open doors, there's a crowd of them behind the doors and they want to come and seize me.[48]

Though Alyosha desires to save Lise from these demons with his love of her, he ironically confesses to the same dream. In contrast to Alyosha, Lise cries out for disorder, murder, and evil: "I want disorder . . . I shall murder somebody . . . I want to do evil."[49] She seems possessed in these moments, revealing the devil's domination of her desires.

In contrast to these fantastical visions of demonic presence, the true presence and activity of the devil in *The Brothers Karamazov* can best be detected through the presence of rivalry among the characters. Leatherbarrow credits the devils with the establishment of their dominion in this world:

> They have recognized that the key to the establishment of 'the kingdom of devils' is to exploit discord and strife in human affairs. Such discord (*раздор*) began with Adam's prioritization of

45. Williams, *Language, Faith and Fiction*, 28.
46. Ibid., 68.
47. Dostoevsky, *The Brothers Karamazov*, 548, 551.
48. Ibid.
49. Ibid., 550.

his own will over that of God, an act that alienated him from the rest of creation; it then continued through the turbulent history of human strife and bloodshed, through the processes of religious schism and fragmentation of belief.[50]

Leatherbarrow's description of the kingdom of devils is reminiscent of Girard's assertion that human society is essentially rivalistic. Beginning with Adam, humans have imitated Satan's contestation of God's authority. This original rivalry between human beings and God has increased manifold, spreading like a disease, so that each person becomes a rival to his or her neighbor.

The demonic feeds off the rivalry between Dmitry and Fyodor, who are oblivious to the devil's delight with their actions. Fyodor supposes devils are harmless superstitions that he mocks but whose toxic effect on him he fails to detect. Williams asserts, "The diabolical is a stage prop for Fyodor, an occasion for mockery or satire, an alibi for his own anarchic cynicism and clownishness."[51] His mockery of the demonic blinds him to the truly demonic character of the bitter rivalries he instigates with his desire for Grushenka. Unable to recognize true goodness in the elder, Fyodor transfers his own hypocrisy to Zosima. He declares, "But I respect him. There's something of Mephistopheles about him."[52] The allusion to Goethe's Mephistopheles shows how Fyodor reduces the devil to a fictional character who is a necessary to counterpoint to the divine.

The meeting with Zosima is full of irony, with each of the characters attempting to transfer their sins onto others or to hide the demons in their hearts. When Dmitry notes about his father's behavior, "Outwardly it's the truth, but inwardly, a lie," he encapsulates the hypocrisy that pervades this entire scene.[53] Despite Zosima's admonishment to Fyodor to act naturally and "not [to] be so ashamed of yourself," Fyodor continues to act the buffoon.[54] He confesses,

> I am an inveterate buffoon, and have been from my birth up, your reverence, it's as though it were a madness in me. I daresay it's a

---

50. Leatherbarrow, *A Devil's Vaudeville*, 181.

51. Williams, *Language, Faith and Fiction*, 65.

52. Dostoevsky, *The Brothers Karamazov*, 123.

53. Ibid., 63.

54. Ibid., 35.

devil within me. But only a little one. A more serious one would have chosen another lodging.[55]

Cognizant of the devil's tools, Zosima cautions Fyodor not to imitate the father of lies: "And the main thing, the very main thing—don't lie."[56] He reproaches Fyodor several times for lying to himself and cautions him against this false behavior. Yet Fyodor continues to choose the devil as his model. He jokingly tells Zosima, "I am the lie and the father of lies. . . . Say, the son of lies, and that will be enough."[57] The butt of the joke is the jokester himself who unwittingly reveals his own diabolic model.

In this "scandalous scene," as Dostoevsky titles the chapter, Fyodor not only participates in demonic farce but also becomes a *skandalon*, or stumbling block. In *I See Satan Fall Like Lightning*, Girard asserts, "Scandals and Satan are fundamentally the same things."[58] The primary difference, according to Girard, is that scandals may be abstract ideas or desired objects, whereas Satan is always a *person*. Moreover, scandals simultaneously attract and repel a person. Girard writes,

> Like the Hebrew word that it translates, "scandal" means, not one of those ordinary obstacles that we avoid easily after we run into it the first time, but a paradoxical obstacle that is almost impossible to avoid: the more this obstacle, or scandal, repels us, the more it attracts.[59]

Fyodor desires to be the buffoon while paradoxically hating himself for acting the buffoon. When Dmitry notes, "All my father wants is scandal," he betrays his own desire for one.[60] All of the Karamazov sons imitate their father, attracted by his scandal while hating the indignity that exists within them. In these early scenes, Dostoevsky emphasizes the failure of Fyodor to

---

55. Ibid., 34.

56. Ibid., 36.

57. Ibid., 37.

58. Girard, *I See Satan*, 45: Girard references Matthew 16:23 where Satan calls Peter both "Satan" and "scandal" within two sentences: "Get behind me, Satan! You are a [*scandal*] stumbling block to me . . ." However, in *Things Hidden Since the Foundation of the World*, Girard also states, "The Cross is the supreme scandal because . . . it discredits and deconstructs all the gods of violence, since it reveals the true God, who has not the slightest violence in him" (429). Girard suggests, then, that scandal and Satan mean the same thing when the stumbling block makes one fall.

59. Ibid., 16.

60. Dostoevsky, *The Brothers Karamazov*, 62.

respond to proper authority, namely that of the elder and monks, and thus to open himself to the demonic.

In contrast to Fyodor, who jests about God and the devil, Ivan defends his own statements of seeming belief to the elder. Ivan protests, "But I wasn't altogether joking."[61] Though Ivan attempts to hide his inner turmoil with an "inexplicable smile," Zosima penetrates his façade and blesses him, "God grant that your heart will attain the answer on earth, and may God bless your path."[62] For Zosima, the answer is radical reliance on God. In this scene, Zosima opposes Fyodor: they represent the two sides of the battle in Ivan's heart between God and Satan. When Ivan earnestly receives the blessing, Fyodor immediately leaps from his seat and points at Ivan, "[T]hat is my son, flesh of my flesh, the dearest of my flesh!"[63] As though claiming territory, Fyodor asserts his oneness with Ivan. Additionally, Fyodor emphasizes his "flesh," a word that biblically connotes sinful nature. Leatherbarrow writes, "Ivan will turn out to be the most significant source of the demonism rife throughout *The Brothers Karamazov*. . . . [H]e is the Karamazov son who, according to Smerdiakov, is most like his corrupt and depraved father."[64]

Whether Ivan actually promotes his proposal to conflate church and state authority, he seems to believe in its underlying assumptions, which Miüsov describes:

> [F]or every individual . . . who does not believe in God or immortality, the moral law of nature must immediately be changed into the exact contrary of the former religious law, and that egoism, even unto crime must become not only lawful but even recognized as the inevitable.[65]

Without the authority of God, Ivan assumes egoism will be the inevitable rule. Surprisingly, Zosima agrees with Ivan's assertion, though the two men have different reactions to the same truth. Zosima knows that when human life is not devoted to God, lawlessness and egoism are the inevitable result, while Ivan later argues that such unbelief is a necessary response to the God who permits innocent suffering. Without God, each person becomes

61. Ibid.
62. Ibid., 61.
63. Ibid.
64. Leatherbarrow, *A Devil's Vaudeville*, 141.
65. Dostoevsky, *The Brothers Karamazov*, 60.

his own authority; yet as Dostoevsky begins to reveal, the authority of the ego serves the devil.

THE DEMONIC NATURE OF
THE GRAND INQUISITOR

Compared to the initial comedy of Fyodor's and Ferapont's diabolic narratives, Ivan's legend of the Grand Inquisitor strikes the reader altogether differently. Following Ivan's accounts of suffering children and his diatribe against God's world, he recites his poem, "The Legend of the Grand Inquisitor." Ivan admits that he has never written the poem down, but he will not refuse Alyosha the honor of being the first listener. In the same mode that Nietzsche adopts in Zarathustra, Ivan tells "The Legend of the Grand Inquisitor" not to discover answers but to propose questions. Ivan cannot explain why he has decided to deliver his poem to Alyosha before it has been written. Rhetorically Ivan asks, "Why should an author forego even one listener?"[66] For Ivan, by authoring the poem, he has assumed control over part of his world. Denis de Rougemont elaborates on the demonic temptation to be an author: "In truth the will to create, the need to write, simply coincides deep down with the Luciferian temptation: to become like God, to make oneself an author, to authorize oneself in an autonomous world."[67] Here, Dostoevsky has incorporated the possibility of both authorial justification before God as well as authorial self-condemnation.

Unlike Dostoevsky as an author, however, Ivan succumbs to demonic temptation. As he narrates his poem to Alyosha, he attempts to control the listener's response. First, he offers a "necessary preface." Then, after he describe Christ's arrival in Seville, he says, "That may be one of the best passages in the poem," interrupting his narrative to demand a specific response from Alyosha.[68] This moment echoes the narratives of Dante's characters in hell who, after relating their stories, demand certain responses from the Pilgrim. Consider for example, Ugolino's admonition, "[I]f you weep not, what can make you weep?"[69] Dostoevsky deliberately resists exercising control over his readers, while Ivan, even in the telling of his poem, appears as authoritarian as his Inquisitor.

66. Dostoevsky, *The Brothers Karamazov*, 227.

67. de Rougemont, *Devil's Share*, 131–32.

68. Dostoevsky, *The Brothers Karamazov*, 229.

69. Dante, *Inferno*, I.xxxiii, 42.

Set in Seville during the Inquisition, the poem begins with the reappearance of Christ, whose first act in the city is to raise a dead child to life.[70] On the previous day, the Grand Inquisitor had burned a hundred heretics, but then Christ enters the scene and reverses such death-dealing by raising persons to life. Fearing that his own authority over life and death has been undermined, the Grand Inquisitor has Christ arrested, and the remainder of the interview is conducted in the prison. According to Victor Terras, the poem's "artificiality and lack of truth shine through in its tacky Gothic romanticism, its sentimental and corny imagery, its overblown rhetorical flourishes, and its self-conscious (and inexact) use of quotation."[71] If Ivan ever attempted to put "The Grand Inquisitor" into print, publishers would likely dismiss the effort as the weak creative attempt of a twenty-three-year-old amateur. Unlike Dostoevsky's own narratives, Ivan's poem lacks the realism of the higher or lower sort, imposes an authorial monologic voice, and misuses rhetorical devices for sentimental effect. Because Satan parodies divine authorship, his acts deviate from perfect beauty, truth, and goodness. The aesthetic deficiency of Ivan's poem suggests demonic imitation of beauty. In style, as in oration and content, Ivan's poem is demonic.

In an issue of *Cross Currents* that O'Connor owned and read, Romano Guardini asserts that the Inquisitor has a "diabolical vision" that hides the "satanic will of attacking God himself," and is thus a representation "which is opposed to the religion of freedom."[72] Guardini focuses on Ivan as the creator of the Grand Inquisitor, conflating his words with Ivan's beliefs. Before delivering his poem, Ivan admits to Alyosha, "I think if the devil doesn't exist, but man has created him, he has created him in his own image and likeness."[73] Ironically, Ivan creates such a "devil" in the Grand Inquisitor who reflects Ivan's own image and likeness. According to Girard, "The diabolical choice of the Inquisitor is nothing else than a reflection of the diabolical choice made by Ivan Karamazov."[74] While Ivan's choice at the

---

70. Ivan has just rehearsed the suffering of children stories from the newspaper and concluded that Christ is ineffectual. Thus, Christ's resurrection of the dead child is especially ironic.

71. Quoted in Leatherbarrow's *A Devil's Vaudeville*, 156.

72. Guardini, "The Legend of the Grand Inquisitor," 61. In her review of Guardini's *The Rosary of Our Lady* (1955), O'Connor attributes the "wealth of cultural background in his spiritual writing" to his knowledge of Dostoevsky (*The Presence of Grace*, 17).

73. Dostoevsky, *The Brothers Karamazov*, 220.

74. Girard, *Resurrection*, 131.

end of the novel is more ambiguous, Girard, like Guardini, underscores the demonic connection between the Inquisitor and Ivan.

Guardini argues that, in the legend, Ivan asserts his deep antagonism toward God's creation. While Ivan believes God's world is inadequate, "the accusation goes even further than that [—] God was not able to create a good world."[75] Ivan essentially demotes God, "declaring him impotent," thus allowing Ivan to establish himself as rival to God's authority.[76] Essentially, in the Grand Inquisitor, Ivan proposes a superman to recreate the world and repair the mistakes of Christ. The Grand Inquisitor admits that he "joined the ranks of those *who have corrected [Christ's] work*."[77] The Inquisitor's haughty declaration echoes Ivan's arrogant desire to remake God's world and to rectify all its imperfections.

The Grand Inquisitor succumbs to the temptation of Peter, before he became the *petros* upon whom Christ built the church. In Matthew 16, Jesus calls Peter a rock, then he reprimands Peter, "Get behind me, Satan! You are a stumbling block to me" (Matt 16:18–23). How did this transformation occur so quickly? Jesus explains his reproach: "[Y]ou do not have in mind the things of God, but the things of men." Peter turned from seeking God's will to seeking his own, and thus transformed himself from a rock of sure faith into a stumbling stone of unbelief, from a follower of Christ into an agent of Satan. De Rougemont elaborates: "[W]hen Peter believes himself the possessor of the good that has been given into his charge, he immediately presumes to administer it to his own ends, as he pleases, not as it has pleased the very Creator of this good."[78] The Grand Inquisitor yields to the same temptation as Peter, having in mind human instead of divine things.

In fitting demonic imitation, Ivan masks his altruistic aims under the cloak of the Grand Inquisitor. He parodies the Catholic Church, speaking as though to Christ, "All has been given by Thee to the Pope,' [the Jesuits] say, 'and all, therefore, is still in the Pope's hands, and there is no need for Thee to come now at all.'"[79] Like Peter, Ivan here renounces Christ's will for his own way. The Grand Inquisitor is a "pope" who will build Christ's church on his own scheme of salvation. He corrects Christ's supposed errors by trading human freedom for a false notion of happiness: "In the end

75. Guardini, "The Legend," 72.
76. Ibid.
77. Dostoevsky, *The Brothers Karamazov*, 240.
78. de Rougemont, *Devil's Share*, 123.
79. Dostoevsky, *The Brothers Karamazov*, 231.

[people] will lay their freedom at our feet, and say to us, 'Make us your slaves, but feed us.'"[80] The Inquisitor argues that humans cannot handle freedom; it causes them suffering. They would rather be controlled and fed than free and hungry. In imitation of the devil, then, the Inquisitor sequesters their freedom in exchange for material comfort.

Yet Dostoevsky hints that the Grand Inquisitor is not himself the ultimate rival authority to God: the Inquisitor submits to Satan's authority by succumbing to the devil's three temptations. In the Gospels, Satan offers Christ miracle, mystery, and authority.[81] According to the Grand Inquisitor, Christ should have accepted these temptations because they would have provided earthly happiness for human beings. Girard writes, "Everything that the proud desire leads them, after all, to prostrate themselves before the *Other*, Satan."[82] Because Satan is the temporary ruler of earth, those who desire only earthly happiness serve Satan. The Grand Inquisitor supplants Christ's image of mother hen from Matthew 23:37 with his own: "[People] will become timid and will look to us and huddle close to us in fear, as chicks to the hen."[83] He notes that the people will "look on us as gods," and he will "deceive them."[84] The Inquisitor insists that the deception is for the good of the people, turning them into lackeys who will be benignly controlled by their masters.

IVAN AND THE DEVIL

While readers may accept the devil's presence in characters such as the Grand Inquisitor, Dostoevsky foresaw they would hesitate to acknowledge the manifested devil. Anticipating his editor's objections to the devil's visit with Ivan, Dostoevsky repeats twice within the same letter that he checked the possibility of such hallucinations with doctors.[85] He records in his notebooks: "THE DEVIL. (A psychological and *detailed* critical explanation of

---

80. Ibid., 232.

81. In Matthew 4:1–11, the three temptations are to turn the stones to bread (miracle), to test God's power by jumping from the roof of the temple (mystery), or to receive authority over the whole world by bowing down before Satan (authority).

82. Girard, *Resurrection*, 125.

83. Dostoevsky, *The Brothers Karamazov*, 239.

84. Ibid., 234.

85. From Matlaw's appendices: Dostoevsky, *The Brothers Karamazov*, 768.

Ivan Fyodorovich and the Devil's appearing.)"[86] The words "psychological" and "critical" indicate Dostoevsky's awareness of his modern audience's trepidation regarding such supernatural phenomena. Dostoevsky's narrator even prefaces Ivan's encounter with a reminder of Ivan's illness:

> I am not a doctor, but yet I feel that the moment has come when I must inevitably give the reader some account of the nature of Ivan Fyodorovich's illness. Anticipating events I can say at least one thing: he was at that moment on the very eve of an attack of brain fever.[87]

Ivan's brain fever provides a rational context for the diabolic encounter and encourages the audience's suspension of disbelief.

After Ivan realizes his own complicity in the murder of his father, the devil appears to him, sitting on his sofa in his apartment, waiting like a friend. Girard indicates that the devil is both "seducer and adversary."[88] Traditionally, he is both

> true and false, illusory and real, fantastic and everyday. Outside of us when we believe him to be in us, he is in us when we believe him outside of us. . . . He offers us a grimacing caricature of what is worst in us.[89]

Dostoevsky's devil thus claims to be illusory, nothing more than a nightmare, but he looks like "a sponger of the best class," a simple gentleman in hand-me-down dress.[90] Dostoevsky describes the devil as wearing clothes from a good tailor probably thrown out by the rich years ago, and with linen too dirty and trousers too tight to be fashionable. His whole ensemble represents his parasitic nature.

This demon's genteel manner cannot obscure his dishonorable position as a "sponger" and a parasite. He confesses his negative condition to Ivan: "Here when I stay with you from time to time, my life gains a kind of reality. . . . What I dream of is becoming incarnate once for all and irrevocably."[91] Girard describes the devil's parasitic nature as "totally

86. Ibid., 769.

87. Dostoevsky, *The Brothers Karamazov*, 601.

88. Girard, *Resurrection*, 131.

89. Ibid.

90. Dostoevsky, *The Brothers Karamazov*, 602.

91. Ibid., 605.

mimetic, which amounts to saying *nonexistent as an individual self*."[92] The devil has no being, as evil is the absence of being. In the same manner as he parodies Christ, he also caricatures God's creatures. The devil identifies himself as "a phantom in life who has lost all beginning and end, and who has even forgotten his own name."[93] Travis Kroeker and Bruce Ward note that this is "a parody of the divine name revealed in Revelation, 'I am the Alpha and Omega, the beginning and the end' (Revelations 1:8; 21:6; 22:13)."[94] Ivan also recognizes the parody, referring to the devil as "only one side of [him]," "of [his] thoughts and feelings, but only the nastiest and stupidest of them."[95] The devil destroys Ivan from within, turning him into a circus mirror reflection of himself, distorted and caricatured.

Beneath the caricature, however, lurks a serious danger, evil skulking in the wings. Dostoevsky's devil resembles the Russian folk *черт*. Simon Franklin describes such a creature as "the shabby, smarmy insinuating demon [that] has an ancient pedigree in Orthodox demonology, and petty demons in general [are] the narrative norm."[96] In a letter to his editor, Dostoevsky demotes his devil to this level: "[I]t's only a devil, a petty devil, and not Satan with 'fallen wings.'"[97] Dostoevsky's devil calls his role in this scheme comedic, though humans take it "as something serious, and that is their tragedy."[98] He indicates the intimate relationship in these scenes between the comic and tragic.

Instead of a fiery, Miltonic vision, Dostoevsky's devil appears as a funny, old Russian gentleman wearing tight, checked trousers, making jokes, and amusing himself with his own speeches. Echoing his author, Ivan too mocks the devil. He tells Alyosha: "He is simply a devil—a paltry, trivial devil. He goes to the baths. If you undressed him, you'd be sure to find he had a tail, long and smooth like a Great Dane's, a yard long, dun color."[99] Ivan's conventional description is reminiscent of Ferapont's and Lise's demons. To reveal the unreality of this figure, Ivan attempts to disrobe and parody the devil.

---

92. Girard, *I See Satan*, 42.

93. Dostoevsky, *The Brothers Karamazov*, 609.

94. Kroeker and Ward, *Remembering the End*, 123.

95. Dostoevsky, *The Brothers Karamazov*, 603–4.

96. Franklin, "Nostalgia for Hell," 47.

97. Dostoevsky, *The Brothers Karamazov*, 768.

98. Ibid., 609.

99. Ibid., 619.

Throughout the devil's discussion with Ivan, the devil jokes and laughs, highlighting the absurdity of this scene. He acts facetiously, relating humorous anecdotes, making plays on words, and mocking his host. For example, when Ivan shouts the Russian expression, "The devil have rheumatism!" the devil responds, "Why not, if I sometimes put on fleshly form? I put on fleshly form and I take the consequences. Satan *sum et nihil humanum a me alienum puto.*"[100] The first joke, in which Satan takes Ivan's remark literally, is overlooked, but Ivan is pleased by the second play on Terence's motto, "I am man, nothing human is alien to me," and the devil soaks up Ivan's pleasure.[101] Then, rambling foolishly, the devil admits his original plan was, "as a joke," to appear "in the figure of a retired general who had served in the Caucasus."[102] Again and again, the devil attempts to make Ivan laugh with these stories. At one point, he is confused about whether Ivan laughs or grows angry: "You are laughing—no, you are not laughing, you are angry."[103] To this remark, Ivan responds with a "smile of hatred."[104] As the smiles and laughs are marked with hate, so the terrible is hidden beneath a comic veneer.

The comic irony in the devil scene highlights Ivan's own inconsistency. Joseph Frank notes, "Dostoevsky's devil . . . does not preach moral sermons but ridicules the inconsistency between Ivan's pangs of conscience and the ideas he has accepted and expounded."[105] Frank sees the conflict in Ivan as primarily one between reason and faith, and Frank underscores the conflict between the abstract and concrete. Ivan cannot actually live out the theories that he has proposed. His idea that "all things are lawful" does not dissipate the guilt incurred when he colludes in an unlawful action. The dialogue with the devil reveals Ivan's inconsistency; he claims to disbelieve in the devil, yet he attempts, like Luther, to strike him with a thrown glass.

"The supreme irony," Frank indicates, "is that it should be the devil who apparently leads [Ivan] along the path to faith."[106] In the worlds of Dostoevsky and O'Connor, the devils are subservient creatures, seeking their own purposes but accomplishing God's instead. In her copy of *The*

100. Ibid., 606.
101. Ibid.
102. Ibid., 614.
103. Ibid., 609.
104. Ibid.
105. Frank, *The Mantle of the Prophet*, 678.
106. Ibid.

Varieties of Religious Experience, O'Connor has underlined William James's reference to a Guido Reni depiction of St. Michael with his foot on Satan's neck. James credits the richness of the picture "to the fiend's figure being there. The richness of its allegorical meaning also is due to his being there—that is, the world is all the richer for having a devil in it, *so long as we keep our foot upon his neck*."[107] Girard offers a similar elaboration on Satan's role in the crucifixion. Because he believes that he is removing the incarnate God from the kingdom of the world, Satan thinks the crucifixion is his victory. However, Christ, in this instance, is not only the scapegoat or sacrifice, he is the High Priest. Thus, the greater plan of the crucifixion—to save all men through one death—could not have been foreseen by Satan. Girard claims, "Only Satan could have set in motion the process of his own destruction without suspecting anything was wrong."[108] In the crucifixion story, Satan dupes himself, and plays into God's hands.

Though the devils in the novels of both Dostoevsky and O'Connor play this important function, the authors never forget and readers should not ignore that he is allowed by God to engage the characters. Ivan's devil admits to serving a higher authority: "So against the grain I serve to produce events and do what's irrational because I am commanded to."[109] The devil asserts that he is commanded to make events happen, but the passive construction leaves the commander undefined. Dostoevsky's devil acknowledges that his methods encourage doubt and increase suffering, but they work to test and increase the faith of believers. Though apparently facetious, the devil relates the truth to Ivan: "I shall sow in you only a tiny grain of faith and it will grow into an oak tree."[110] In fact, the devil does test Ivan's bit of faith in a "crucible of doubt," as Ivan begins questioning his motives for unmasking Smerdyakov. Williams writes that this devil continually keeps us "aware of our complex motivations and of the ambiguity of appearances (ourselves to ourselves, as well as the world to our minds)."[111] Unintentionally, the devil accomplishes God's work in Ivan.

The extent of Ivan's transition from rebellion to faith remains ambiguous even at the conclusion of the novel. Directly after his encounter, Ivan

107. Quoted in Kinney's *Flannery O'Connor's Library*, 32.

108. Girard, *I See Satan*, 151.

109. Dostoevsky, *The Brothers Karamazov*, 609.

110. Ibid., 612.

111. Williams, *Language, Faith and Fiction*, 72.

realizes that the devil "was not a dream, it all happened just now!"[112] To Alyosha, he asserts the reality of the devil, confessing that the devil knows both Ivan's pride and his cowardice about witnessing in the court. Looking at Ivan sleeping at the end of this scene, Alyosha reflects, "God, in Whom [Ivan] disbelieved, and His truth were gaining mastery over his heart, which still refused to submit."[113] Though not prepared for absolute submission to a divine authority, Ivan confesses publicly to his moral culpability in his father's murder. Aware of his pride and his cowardice as revealed to him by the devil inside him, and still skeptical of virtue, Ivan nonetheless acts virtuously.

When Ivan walks into the courtroom, he is described as moving slowly "looking at no one, and with his head bowed, as though in gloomy thought."[114] In these few moments, he attempts to overcome the devil inside of him. After consistently answering in the negative, Ivan finally asserts that he knows the true murderer Smerdyakov: "It was he, not my brother, who killed our father. He murdered him and I incited him to do it. . . . Who doesn't desire his father's death?"[115] While everyone believes him to be deranged, Ivan insists on publicly confessing. He even testifies to the reality of the devil, though this admission sends the court into hysterics. Clutching his head, Ivan yells, "Have you any water? Give me a drink for Christ's sake!"[116] First, the water may allude to Christ on the Cross, who cried out in thirst. Second, the mention of Christ himself suggests Ivan's move towards God. Here, Ivan's action foretells potential redemption for his character.

While Ivan lies unconscious from his brain fever, in the next room, Alyosha and Katerina Ivanovna debate his condition. Katya calls him a "hero of honor and conscience" because he "sacrificed himself for his brother" by plotting Dmitry's escape before his conviction.[117] Apparently, Ivan sought out Katya, though he believed her to be in love with Dmitry, and provided her with money to help Dmitry escape. Katya exclaims to Alyosha, "Oh, [Ivan] foresaw his illness! He told me that . . . if he died or was taken dangerously ill, I was to save Mitya alone. . . . Oh, that was

112. Dostoevsky, *The Brothers Karamazov*, 617.

113. Ibid., 622.

114. Ibid., 650.

115. Ibid., 651.

116. Ibid., 652.

117. Ibid., 717.

a sacrifice!"[118] In Katya's view, Ivan's final acts before his madness imitate Christ's self-sacrifice. Though neither the outcome nor any signs of hope are given, both Alyosha and Katya continue to speak not about Ivan's final damnation but about his physical and spiritual recovery. The hope at the end of this story is founded then on Ivan's actions prior to his illness and confinement.

THE DEMONIC IN O'CONNOR'S WORK

Because of O'Connor's emphasis on and preoccupation with evil, critics such as John Hawkes and André Bleikasten accuse her of being in the devil's camp and offering a false sense of grace. For instance, Bleikasten writes:

> In O'Connor, grace is not effusion but aggression. It is God's violence responding to Satan's violence, divine counter terror fighting the mutiny of evil. The operations of the divine and of the demonic are so disturbingly alike that the concept of God suggested by her work is in the last resort hardly more reassuring than her devil.[119]

Here, Bleikasten accuses O'Connor of presenting good and evil too equally, as if she were an outright Manichean. Yet O'Connor does not view this relationship between the two forces. For her, Satan's violence responds to God's grace, and the devil "is always accomplishing ends other than his own."[120] O'Connor writes, "In my stories a reader will find that the devil accomplishes a good deal of groundwork that seems to be necessary before grace is effective. . . . This is another mystery."[121] The mystery in O'Connor's stories, as in Dostoevsky's novel, is that, ironically, the demonic is used to effect grace.

This either-or choice involving the divine and the demonic has been identified as the central controversy of both Dostoevsky's and O'Connor's fiction. "Believe Jesus or the devil!" the preacher Bevel Summers calls out in O'Connor's "The River." He demands, "Testify to one or the other!"[122] Preston M. Browning Jr. declares that this imperative is "central to Flannery O'Connor's art, and it should be noted that Miss O'Connor was ada-

118. Ibid., 718.

119. Bleikasten, "The Heresy of Flannery O'Connor," 153.

120. O'Connor, *The Habit of Being*, 367.

121. O'Connor, *Mystery and Manners*, 117.

122. O'Connor, *Collected Works*, 163.

mant about her belief in the devil as a real, concrete being."[123] Several of O'Connor's descriptions of the demonic resemble Dostoevsky's, especially her emphasis on its reality, and most particularly her stress on demonic authority of the autonomous self.

When O'Connor began *The Violent Bear It Away*, she conceived an ensemble resembling *The Brothers Karamazov*: "a old man, three sons, and a bastard grandson."[124] She eventually whittled the story down to an old man, his nephew Rayber, Rayber's son Bishop, and the old man's great-nephew Tarwater. Though four characters dominate the action of the plot, only one character—Tarwater—stands at the axis of choice between following God or Satan. His two rival guardians Mason Tarwater and Rayber, who both want to adopt him and teach him how to model his life after them, represent the different metaphysical models: Mason is a prophet of God and Rayber the schoolteacher is, according to the narrator, "like the devil," though not intentionally a demonic agent. As in *The Brothers Karamazov* the demonic here is present from the beginning and climaxes with the actual appearance of the devil.[125]

In *Desire, Violence, & Divinity in Modern Southern Fiction*, Gary Ciuba undertakes a Girardian reading of *The Violent Bear It Away*. He describes the model-disciple triangle relationship between Mason Tarwater, Rayber, and young Tarwater. Detailing the various stumbling block references and their meaning in the novel, Ciuba calls the novel itself a "prolonged obstacle course."[126] In *Things Hidden Since the Foundation of the World*, Girard defines biblical scandal as "the model exerting its special form of temptation, causing attraction to the extent that it is an obstacle and forming an obstacle to the extent that it can attract."[127] Ciuba shows how the two models in *The Violent Bear It Away*, Mason and Rayber, both attract and repel Tarwater. Ciuba does not align Mason and Rayber with the metaphysical sides that they represent, but his description of them as rival authorities parallels Girard's account of the either-or between God and Satan.

Tarwater struggles between the rival authorities of his Great-Uncle Mason and his Uncle Rayber. Ciuba notes Tarwater's connection to both

123. Browning Jr., "Flannery O'Connor's Devil Revisited," 326.

124. Driggers, Dunn, and Gordon, *Manuscripts*, 78.160a. pp 1–7, T. em O'C, T, i, pencil.

125. O'Connor, *Collected Works*, 365.

126. Ciuba, *Desire, Violence, & Divinity*, 118.

127. Girard, *Things Hidden*, 416.

models; he writes, "Tarwater is Mason's disciple in spite of himself" and "Tarwater and Rayber grow so much to resemble each other that any apparent mark of difference is just a momentary pause on the whirligig of mimesis."[128] While Rayber sees the old man inside Tarwater, the narrator finds resemblances between Rayber and Tarwater. In fact, Tarwater himself models Rayber, which he acknowledges when he shouts, "My great-uncle is dead and burnt, just like you would have burnt him yourself!"[129] Tarwater tries not to model either Mason or Rayber, yet in this unsuccessful attempt to be his own authority, he models the devil.

When Mason dies, young Tarwater must decide whether to return to Rayber, and a stranger's voice weighs in on his decision. "'Now I can do anything I want to,' [Tarwater] said, softening the stranger's voice so that he could stand it."[130] There is something malicious about the voice that Tarwater initially resists; he tries to lessen its grating effect. Yet the voice is intimately tied up with his own thoughts. First, the voice advises him to be his own authority, to "do anything" that he wants to do. The voice deceives him into believing that he is self-authorized, even though it commands him to follow. For instance, "his friend" suggests to "Go take look at [Mason] and see if he's fell off his chair," and the boy quickly does so.[131] The friend or stranger, as Tarwater refers to him, is the actual authority. Smerdyakov's description of Ivan sounds like an accurate assessment of Tarwater; when he says to Ivan, "[Y]ou're very proud. . . . [Not] having to bow to anyone— that's what you most care about."[132] Ironically, in the same way that Ivan's pride leaves him prostrate before the devil so does Tarwater's pride invoke his inner demon. Ciuba declares that O'Connor's subjective narrator has misnamed Tarwater's stranger: "Far from being alien and unknown, he is Tarwater's twin."[133] Tarwater hosts a demonic double inside his mind, and convinced of his own authority, he follows this demon's orders.

Like Dostoevsky, O'Connor introduces her devil in a natural context and yet desires that her audience perceive his supernatural reality. Cognizant of her audience's likelihood to hesitate at acknowledging the supernatural, O'Connor admits to writing specifically for those who no longer

128. Ciuba, *Desire, Violence, & Divinity*, 227, 134.

129. O'Connor, *Collected Works*, 386.

130. Ibid., 345.

131. Ibid., 353.

132. Dostoevsky, *The Brothers Karamazov*, 599.

133. Ciuba, *Desire, Violence, & Divinity*, 141.

believe in the devil. She says that her own fiction shows "the action of grace in territory held largely by the devil [and] what I write is read by an audience which puts little stock either in grace or the devil."[134] Thus, in *The Violent Bear It Away* O'Connor attempts to develop her devil's credibility by placing him initially as a face and voice in Tarwater's mind, referring to him as the "stranger":

> [Tarwater] didn't search out the stranger's face but he knew by now that it was sharp and friendly and wise. . . . He had lost his dislike for the thought of the voice. Only every now and then it sounded like the stranger's voice to him.[135]

Though readers may reduce her stranger to a psychological abnormality, O'Connor clarified her intentions to John Hawkes (Nov. 20, 1959), "I want to be certain that the Devil gets identified as the Devil and not simply taken for this or that psychological tendency."[136]

Rationally, the devil may be explained as the product of Tarwater's inner turmoil, at least at the beginning of the novel. However, the devil in *The Violent Bear It Away*, like the devil of Scripture, is legion. He appears first in Tarwater's mind, then in the person of Meeks, often in Rayber's voice, and finally in the lavender-suited rapist. Ciuba writes, "Seen so often, the stranger casts a hallucinatory aura over *The Violent Bear It Away* so that everywhere there is mimicked and mirrored his two-faced look."[137] As in *The Brothers Karamazov*, demonic presence permeates *The Violent Bear It Away*.

Often considered by critics and by O'Connor herself[138] as a precursor to the final demonic driver, Meeks the copper flue salesman picks up Tarwater as a hitchhiker after Tarwater burns his uncle's property. O'Connor describes Meeks as a "thin fellow with a narrow face that appeared to have been worn down to the sharpest possible depressions."[139] A careful craftswoman with her diction, O'Connor denotes want and lack in her depiction

---

134. O'Connor, *Mystery and Manners*, 118.

135. O'Connor, *Collected Works*, 352.

136. O'Connor, *The Habit of Being*, 360.

137. Ciuba, *Desire, Violence, & Divinity*, 144.

138. O'Connor, *The Habit of Being*, 359, to John Hawkes, 20 Nov., 1959: "I had meant for Meeks and the pervert at the end to take on the form of Tarwater's Friend, and when I had set out I had in mind that Rayber would echo all his friend's sentiments in a form that the reader would identify himself with . . . made him a caricature."

139. O'Connor, *Collected Works*, 352.

with words such as "thin," "narrow," and "depression." Thus, she connects Meeks's appearance with demonic privation. Moreover, the sharpness of Meeks's face recalls medieval engravings of devils with pointed chins. Meeks wears a hat "used by business men who would like to look like cowboys" in order to suggest his counterfeit nature.[140] Though not intentionally in demonic service, Meeks imitates the devil in his attempt to corrupt Tarwater. Similar to Rayber's misuse of the term "Charity," Meeks blabbers about "love" without meaning *agape* or *caritas*. For Meeks, "love" equals sentimentality or false sincerity: "[I]t had been his personal experience that you couldn't sell a copper flue to a man you didn't love. . . . He said love was the only policy that worked 95% of the time."[141] Meeks's form of love is not an end in itself but a means to sell flues. He falsifies compassion to use people, as he advises Tarwater, "And that's the way it ought to be in this world—nobody owing nobody nothing."[142] Like Tarwater's stranger, Meeks proposes self-centeredness and self-authority.

While Meeks heralds the appearance of Tarwater's stranger, Rayber is the demonic echo. Rayber has his counterpart in O'Connor's "The Lame Shall Enter First," where a psychiatrist named Sheppard has a son Norton with whom he has little relationship, and so he seeks to educate a belligerent juvenile delinquent named Rufus Johnson. O'Connor considered the story a failure because, as she writes to John Hawkes (Feb. 6, 1962), "In this one [story], I'll admit that the Devil's voice is my own."[143] Hawkes's theory was that O'Connor, like Blake's Milton, was of the Devil's party[144] without knowing it. A few months before this letter to Hawkes, she defended herself as not being a secret sympathizer with the Devil. She writes (Nov. 28, 1961) that the story is "about one of Tarwater's terrible cousins, a lad named Rufus Johnson, and it will add fuel to your theory."[145] In the same way that Rayber believes he can save Tarwater through education, Sheppard believes he will save Rufus Johnson. He tries to overcome the foolishness of his

---

140. Ibid., 362.

141. Ibid.

142. Ibid., 362.

143. O'Connor, *The Habit of Being*, 464.

144. Ibid., 359, letter to John Hawkes, 20 Nov., 1959: "I had meant for Meeks and the pervert at the end to take on the form of Tarwater's Friend, and when I had set out I had in mind that Rayber would echo all his friend's sentiments in a form that the reader would identify himself with . . . made him a caricature."

145. O'Connor, *Collected Works*, 456.

grandfather's faith, suggesting, "Maybe I can explain your devil to you."[146] Because Rufus is more intelligent than Sheppard's own son, Sheppard holds him in higher regard. Sheppard mimics Satan, and so Rufus appropriately accuses him, "Satan has you in his power."[147] O'Connor's story ends with Sheppard's sudden turn from the demonic which he sees "leering at him from the eyes of Johnson."[148]

When O'Connor then gives the devil credit for "The Lame Shall Enter First," or admits to "giving the devil his due" with Rayber, she highlights her own difficulty in depicting these characters.[149] For O'Connor, creating Rayber was a "stumbling block," as she admits to John Hawkes (Oct. 6, 1959): "I spent most of the seven years on Rayber."[150] Ciuba writes, "In stumbling over Rayber, O'Connor was feeling what it was like to be blocked by the kind of negative double that continually captivates all of her models and disciples in *The Violent Bear It Away*."[151] Though she failed with Sheppard, O'Connor overcomes the problem with Rayber. In other manuscripts of *The Violent Bear It Away* Rayber smiles at the drowning of his son, but O'Connor leaves the ending more ambiguous. She writes (Oct. 31, 1959), "I would have liked for [Rayber] to be saved, and it is ambiguous whether he may be or not."[152] By allowing for the possibility of redemption, O'Connor keeps Rayber from being reduced to a caricature of the demonic.

Rayber should not be conflated with the devil, but he does mimic him. Aping Christ, as the devil does, Rayber tells Tarwater, "You need to be saved right here now from the old man and everything he stands for. And I'm the one who can save you."[153] O'Connor's narrator describes him ironically as a "fanatical country preacher," though Rayber attempts to be anything but a preacher.[154] Rayber desires to provide Tarwater salvation through an intellectual enlightenment: "[G]etting out from under the old man is just like coming out of the darkness into the light."[155] In these words, Rayber

---

146. Ibid., 601.

147. O'Connor, *The Habit of Being*, 477.

148. O'Connor, *Collected Works*, 632.

149. O'Connor, *The Habit of Being*, 352.

150. Ibid., 353.

151. Ciuba, *Desire, Violence, & Divinity*, 128.

152. O'Connor, *The Habit of Being*, 357.

153. O'Connor, *Collected Works*, 438.

154. Ibid.

155. Ibid., 389.

twists John 1:9 where Christ is called the "true light that gives light to every man." Rayber misidentifies the light, for 1 John 2:10 declares, "Whoever loves his brother lives in the light and there is nothing in him to make him stumble." Rayber struggles to love his nephew. He feels divided between his rational self and his violent self, though the two selves are sides of the same self. Against his rational self, the "violent self incline[s] him to see the boy [Tarwater] as an enemy and he [knows] that nothing would hinder his progress with the case so much as giving into such an inclination."[156] Despite his rational approach to his violent longings, Rayber objectifies Tarwater, calling him a "case" and focusing more on his own "progress" than on the good of Tarwater. Ciuba describes Rayber as the most violent of the characters: "Rayber ultimately believes in the divinity of violence that he imagines himself as foreswearing."[157] At one point Rayber even attempts to drown his son Bishop. Rayber's violent desires betray not only that he lives in darkness, but that by choosing such darkness, he imitates Satan.

In "The Partridge Festival," the main character mimics Satan by parodying Christ's words. Calhoun, who is writing an exposé on a mass murderer, says, "Know the truth [. . .] and the truth shall make you free."[158] Yet Calhoun will not uncover the "truth" but decide it, for he and Mary Elizabeth have convinced themselves that the mass murderer named Singelton is a man "who is willing to suffer for the right to be himself."[159] Guided by their misconception of justice, which to them means the right of an individual to be himself, the two undertake a trip to visit Singelton in the state mental hospital. As they approach the hospital where Singelton is committed, Mary Elizabeth quotes Dante, unaware of the spiritual truth behind her words. She says, "Abandon all hope ye who enter here," not realizing that the hell they are approaching is embodied in Singelton himself.[160]

For both of them, Singelton is a superman who has been victimized by the weak townspeople. Mary Elizabeth even brings *Thus Spake Zarathustra* to him, expecting him to be a Nietzschean hero. To be permitted to visit him, they pretend to be his "kin." Unfortunately, Singelton is not a man-god but a madman who leers lustfully at Mary Elizabeth and who flashes his naked body before both of them. This encounter with an evil one impels

---

156. Ibid., 417.

157. Ciuba, *Desire, Violence, & Divinity*, 131.

158. O'Connor, *Collected Works*, 424.

159. Ibid., 423.

160. Ibid., 439.

them to flee from the room—the truth has been exposed. On June 22, 1961, O'Connor informs John Hawkes that Singleton is "one of those devils who go about piercing pretensions, not the devil who goes about like a roaring lion seeking whom he may devour."[161] Rather than follow the policy for concealment, this demon enjoys "the pleasing results of direct terrorism," as Lewis puts it in *The Screwtape Letters*.[162] This stunt would place Singleton on the lower rung of O'Connor's "hierarchy of devils."[163]

While Calhoun and Mary Elizabeth escape violation by the devil that they toyed with, Tarwater encounters a devouring devil. Ciuba writes, "Having allowed this double to possess his soul when he did violence to Bishop, the fourteen year old finds that his consort now return to posses his flesh in erotic violation."[164] The young Tarwater is victimized in the flesh by the evil one whom he has allowed to victimize his soul. As long as the devil remained merely a voice inside his head, it could be conflated with his own authority. However, when the devil is manifested in a person and takes sexual advantage of the drugged and unconscious Tarwater, the reader understands the demonic identity of the voice.

In *The Brothers Karamazov* the devil has visited Ivan several times before the encounter that the reader witnesses, so in *The Violent Bear It Away* the devil's visits increase slowly into this full reality—as if O'Connor were recalling Dostoevsky's tactic. Ivan first indicates his history with the devil by defining the cold he feels when entering the room as "a recollection, or more exactly, a reminder of something agonizing and revolting that was in that room now, at that moment, and had been there before."[165] Foreseeing this encounter, Ivan smiles with angry anticipation as though confronting a well-known foe. He informs the devil, "You won't drive me to fury as you did *last time*" and in the same paragraph refers again to "last time": "I sometimes don't see you and don't even hear your voice as I did *last time*, but I always guess at what you are prating."[166] He twice mentions a previous encounter to which the reader has not been privy. Dostoevsky suggests that the encounters may have begun with the devil as only a voice and developed into the full form now experienced. Through Ivan's experience

161. O'Connor, *The Habit of Being*, 443.

162. Lewis, *Screwtape*, 31.

163. O'Connor, *The Habit of Being*, 443.

164. Ciuba, *Desire, Violence, & Divinity*, 155.

165. Dostoevsky, *The Brothers Karamazov*, 601.

166. Ibid., 603, writer's emphasis.

with the devil, Dostoevsky emphasizes how evil intensifies, how it becomes more and more expected, and ultimately dominates more and more of a person's existence.

Analogously, O'Connor's devil in *The Violent Bear It Away* also develops, progressing from a vague face and strange voice to violet eyes constantly piercing Tarwater to full embodiment in the lavender-suited man. When Tarwater climbs into the stranger's car, "an unpleasant sensation that he [can] not place [comes] over him," as he recognizes this paradoxically familiar stranger.[167] Tarwater thinks, "There was something familiar to him in the look of the stranger but he could not place where he had seen him before."[168] Like the stranger in Tarwater's mind, this stranger also wears a panama hat. At the beginning of the novel, the hat obscures the stranger's eyes, but when Tarwater drowns Bishop, he beholds their violet color. The driver, too, has violet eyes, though O'Connor describes them here as "the same color as his shirt," as well as the same color of his car.[169] O'Connor calls him "old-looking young man," projecting onto him a timeless quality, but she also makes him like the living dead with pale skin and "deep hollows under his cheekbones."[170] Like Dostoevsky's old Russian gentleman, this figure resembles a parasite. Furthermore, like Dostoevsky's devil, O'Connor's devil is ridiculous, appearing in a lavender suit that coordinates with his lavender-colored car. He speaks colloquially, using "shaw" and "ain't," rambling on superfluously, also like Dostoevsky's devil, enamored with his own voice.

Both stories acknowledge the devil "could take on any look that suited him."[171] Earlier, Dostoevsky's devil mentions he could have come as a general, so why does Tarwater's devil come in this manner? The seemingly simple, yet venomous, statements by the devil reveal the purpose for his form. For example, when he foolishly says to Tarwater, "That's all a prophet is good for—to admit somebody else is an ass or a whore," he is playing off Tarwater's own desire to avoid prophecy.[172] Dostoevsky's devil treats Ivan similarly, repeating his own thoughts back to him. While Dostoevsky and O'Connor each portray a devil who is, as Dorothy Sayers writes in "The

---

167. O'Connor, *Collected Works*, 469.
168. Ibid.
169. Ibid.
170. Ibid.
171. Ibid., 365.
172. Ibid., 355.

Faust Legend and the Idea of the Devil," "ultimately a fool as well as a villain," each devil is only as foolish and villainous as its host.[173]

While Tarwater focuses throughout the novel on avoiding the contrary summons of his models, he ultimately imitates them both. Therefore, after he accepts only himself and thereby unknowingly adopts the devil as his model, the self-deceived Tarwater becomes more demonic. He has convinced himself that could be his own authority, but these lies have encouraged the demonic presence within him to the extent that, in a moment of demonic imitation, he drowns Bishop. Ciuba notes, "Whereas the youth imitates Mason's desire in wanting to baptize Bishop, he comes to mimic Rayber's desire in wanting to kill Bishop."[174] Ultimately, Tarwater models not only Mason but also Rayber; he cannot escape his models and their influence.

Similarly, in "The Comforts of Home" Thomas deceives himself into believing that he is his own authority. However, he is possessed by the demonic, who disguises himself as the ghost of Thomas's father. As reasonable as Ivan or Rayber, Thomas considers his mother's charity toward a suicidal teenage girl as irrational: "She proceeded always from the tritest considerations . . . into the most foolhardy engagements with the devil, whom, of course, she never recognized."[175] O'Connor's narrator follows this assessment with an observation: "The devil for Thomas was a manner of speaking."[176] Here, Thomas has hold of the wrong devil. Like Tarwater deceiving himself, Thomas has duped himself. Moreover, like Fyodor, he revels in demonic parody: "But when virtue got out of hand with her, as now, a sense of devils grew upon him, and these were not mental quirks in himself or the old lady, they were denizens with personalities, present though not visible, who might any moment be expected to shriek or rattle a pot."[177] Thomas, then, who believes in moderate good and evil, mixes modern rationalism with comic appreciation of caricatured demons.

When Thomas's mother adopts the orphaned teen Sarah Ham, who calls herself Star Drake, his father's voice begins haunting him. Though Thomas "had not been able to endure [his father] in life," a fact that reveals his rejection of parental authority, he follows the authoritative directions

173. Sayers, "The Faust Legend and the Idea of the Devil," 174.
174. Ciuba, *Desire, Violence, & Divinity*, 133.
175. O'Connor, *Collected Works*, 575.
176. Ibid.
177. Ibid., 576.

of his father's ghost.[178] Thomas reveals his openness to demonic possession when he absentmindedly "ask[s] himself what the attitude of God was
to this, meaning if possible to adopt it."[179] The phrase lays itself open to
ambiguity: could he be considering how to imitate God rather than parody
him? However, Thomas follows this thought with a list of ways to "get rid"
of Sarah Ham, revealing the triumph of demonic sovereignty.

Moreover, like Ivan's and Tarwater's devils who begin as voices and
gain strength, so too does Thomas's father gain presence. At first merely a
voice in Thomas's head, the old man "appeared to have taken up his station
in Thomas's mind and from there, usually squatting, he shot out the same
rasping suggestion."[180] Superficially, it is interesting that the man wears a
panama hat, as does Tarwater's devil. O'Connor describes him in further
detail as "small, wasp-like, in his yellowed panama hat, his seersucker suit,
his pink carefully-soiled shirt, his small string tie." By this point in the story,
Thomas has submitted to his "father," the demon in his head, and he has
visited the sheriff and attempted to hide a pistol in the girl's handbag. In
devising this fraudulent scheme, the demon-possessed Thomas follows his
father's command to fire the gun. In this deadly action, Thomas reveals his
true father, the father of lies, who was a murderer from the beginning.

Those who have courted the devil discover his violence. After Tarwater is sexually victimized, he sets the ground on fire "until the fire was
eating greedily at the evil ground, burning every spot the stranger could
have touched."[181] This purging of evil by fire recalls Deuteronomy 4:24: "For
the Lord your God is a consuming fire, a jealous God." Over the course
of the narrative, Tarwater has been struggling between choosing God or
Satan and now, in imitation of the true God, he burns out the enemy and is
refined by fire. Running out from the burning woods, he sees immediately
the "road home, ground that had been familiar to him since his infancy
but now it looked like strange and alien country."[182] Tarwater is returning
home, becoming again like a child, yet a new child. The world looks different because he has received revelation: "His scorched eyes no longer looked
hollow. . . . They looked as if, touched with a coal like the lips of the prophet,

178. Ibid., 577.
179. Ibid., 580.
180. Ibid., 585.
181. Ibid., 472.
182. Ibid., 473.

they would never be used for ordinary sights again."[183] Now accepting his call to be a prophet, Tarwater's eyes changed. As Buford notices, "Nothing seemed alive about the boy but his eyes . . . [which] appeared to see something coming in the distance."[184] He has prophetic vision. Like his uncle before him who would wander in the woods and return with "fire in his eyes," so Tarwater now has such a fire burning within him.[185]

Previously, Tarwater had replaced his great-uncle's authority with his own authority. Now he throws himself to the ground, and he listens to the divine command: "GO WARN THE CHILDREN OF GOD OF THE TERRIBLE SPEED OF MERCY."[186] The command is not shouted at him, but comes as quietly as the voice that whispered to Elijah. In imitation of Moses, another Old Testament prophet, Tarwater smears dirt from his great-uncle's grave like ashes upon his forehead, and walks forward "without looking back."[187] The commandment not to look back is given to Lot and his family in Genesis. Tarwater's mission is to imitate not merely the prophets before him, but more importantly to reveal the fatherhood of God by awakening all of the sleeping "children of God" to their true parenthood.[188]

CONCLUSION

Dostoevsky and O'Connor create devils that are not merely psychological hallucinations or base self-reflections, but rather nonentities who receive their negative being by feeding off willing hosts such as Ivan and Tarwater. Yet at the same time that these characters comply with the devil, they also oppose him. While the devil attempts to mask his existence, his hosts reveal him, even if inadvertently. O'Connor and Dostoevsky unmask the devil who has hidden under the guise of the triumphant and omnipotent self. In Girardian terms, Satan is the "mimetic contagion itself."[189] However, he has a name and an identity more than being "an impersonal principle."[190] Before Christ, he held a list of pagan titles; now the Gospels have accurately

183. Ibid.
184. Ibid., 477.
185. Ibid., 334.
186. Ibid., 478.
187. Ibid.
188. Ibid.
189. Girard, *I See Satan*, 69.
190. Ibid.

titled him "the prince of this world" for he "is the absence of being" that inspires our false desires, rivalries, and the illusion of autonomy.[191] When Dostoevsky and O'Connor depict such an entity, they must hold a mirror to a blind audience, who would not recognize the devil, even if he appeared before their face, especially not in their own reflections. Recognizing the devil as a true descriptor of experience, Dostoevsky and O'Connor create real terrors, rather than symbols, which reveal the demonic model for selfish desires. By showing readers his face in their novels, Dostoevsky and O'Connor hope to expose the devil and moreover all his evil tricks.

191. Ibid.

CONCLUSION

IMITATING THE SON
AND THE KINGDOM OF LOVE

FYODOR DOSTOEVSKY AND FLANNERY O'Connor are more than gargoyles posing on a cathedral scaring away devils; they also, with portraits of Christlike love, direct readers' eyes upwards like the spirals of the Sagrada Familia. As mimetic artists, they believe in the potential for stories to transform readers. They create characters who imitate Christ in the hopes that such imitation may inspire further mimesis. While the demonic looms large in their fiction, they only allow him enough reins as to accomplish—unknowingly—God's work. For the stories to portray accurately the imitation of Christ, there must be the free choice available to their characters. The choice to submit to divine or demonic authority does not present itself only once, nor is it merely a choice between two actions with succeeding consequences. Rather the choice requires a lifelong commitment to one of two radically alternative ways of living: denounce God because suffering exists in this world and thus perpetuate human violence or embrace the reality of suffering and discover a life of love and freedom.

TWO TYPES OF VIOLENCE

According to René Girard, only Christ can free human beings from the cycle of violence in which we have enslaved ourselves because only Christ saw through the myths about violence and suffering. Since Cain's murder of Abel, humans have perpetually engaged in cycles of mimetic rivalry that culminate in murder. Yet each generation denies its violent nature, refuses to see its culpability, and thus reproduces its successor's mistakes. Girard explains, "The *sons* believe they can express their independence of the *fathers* by condemning them, that is, by claiming to have no part in the murder. But by virtue of this very fact, they unconsciously imitate and repeat the acts of their fathers."[1] Ironically, the sons imitate their fathers in the very attempt not to model them.

Girard's theory is that poor modeling has a domino effect: children model Satan because they model their parents who modeled Satan. Every child inherits the sins of the parent, including the lie that denies such inheritance. Neither father nor the son admits guilt, and so the violence continues. Girard convicts everyone: "To be a son of Satan is the same thing as being the son of those whose have killed their prophets since the foundation of the world."[2] Satan enslaves people with the falsehood that they have not sinned, and that they have no blood on their hands. Dostoevsky's Ivan and O'Connor's Rayber, for example, live as though they are exempt from such violence: both deny their responsibility in the murder of their father and son, respectively.

To expose this falsehood, O'Connor and Dostoevsky narrate tales that act as illumining mirrors to such satanic deceit. Dostoevsky shows that Ivan's hate for his father Fyodor is a deflected desire to slay God the Father. When Smerdyakov kills Fyodor, Dostoevsky demonstrates Ivan's complicity in this parricidal and theological murder. In O'Connor's "The Comforts of Home," the son Thomas, like Ivan, does not consider himself a violent person, yet his hate towards Sarah Ham intensifies until he fires a gun at her. Unfortunately, Thomas unintentionally shoots his mother, and the violent accident betrays his parricidal impulse. Following in Dostoevsky's footsteps, O'Connor illustrates Girard's assertion, "Not to love one's brother and to kill him are the same thing."[3] In their fiction, both Dostoevsky and O'Connor attempt to exhibit the violent consequences of rejecting the divine as Father.

In a foreword to a collection of excerpts that reveal the gospel in Dostoevsky's oeuvre, Malcolm Muggeride rephrases the choice for God over

---

1. Girard, *Things Hidden,* 160.
2. Ibid., 161.
3. Ibid., 214.

the devil in these terms, "Accept suffering and be redeemed by it."[4] After Ivan lines up his evidence against God, listing seemingly endless brutalities against children, he declines any offer of redemption. In so doing, Ivan surrenders to an oppositional kingdom, one of satanic destruction, instead of that of God's love. Girard explains that this refusal means Ivan is "refusing the knowledge that Jesus bears—refusing the knowledge of violence and all its works."[5] Ironically, the Karamazov who most prides himself on his intellect chooses ignorance about this matter. While Ivan unwittingly adopts citizenship in the kingdom of violence, he soon discovers Satan is its dictator. His painful encounters with a devil propel him into madness, but it proves to be a madness of purgation. The hope for Ivan rests in the biblical epigraph to the novel, "Verily, verily, I say unto you, except a corn of wheat fall into the ground and die, it abideth alone: but if it die, it bringeth forth much fruit" (John 12:24). If Ivan's seed has fallen here, then there is hope for him yet to bear spiritual fruit.

O'Connor counters the nihilistic violence exemplified by Ivan with violent intrusions of divine grace. While some critics of O'Connor conflate moments of revelation in her fiction as a side effect of a violent situation with the spiritual violence enacted by God, there is a significant difference. In *The Violent Bear It Away* Tarwater accepts grace after his rape by the demonic man with purple eyes, however, God does not cause the violence in this instance. O'Connor seems to be saying, hyperbolically, if you court the devil, you're going to get raped. In response to this discovery, Tarwater finally, for the plans of God, relinquishes his desire for self-design. Contrasting with this human or demonic violence, O'Connor shows in the same novel, God burning away Mason's rage. Mason initiates his ministry by furiously preaching the destruction of the world, then one morning "the destruction he had been waiting for had fallen in his own brain and his own body."[6] The wounding revelation purges Mason of his violence; this spiritual violence represents how God acts in O'Connor's fiction.

O'Connor draws her title for *The Violent Bear It Away* from Matthew 11:12, "The kingdom of God suffers violence, and the violent bear it away." Biblical scholars offer various interpretations of this passage, attempting to account for a nonviolent God's seeming affirmation here of violence. According to O'Connor, the "violent" of whom Christ speaks are ascetics

4. Muggeridge, "Foreword," *The Gospel in Dostoyevsky*.

5. Girard, *Things Hidden*, 208.

6. O'Connor, *Collected Works*, 332.

(March 16, 1960): "That this [verse] is [about] the violence of love, of giving more than the law demands of an asceticism like John the Baptist's . . . —all this is overlooked."[7] In the novel, Tarwater initially rejects Christ, and when he murders Bishop, he succumbs to demonic temptation—yet divine grace acts even through Tarwater's violent rejection of it, for the misguided teen also baptizes Bishop while drowning him. Following his rape, Tarwater is purged of demonic possession. He joins the tradition of John the Baptist, accepting the violence that he will inevitably encounter by preaching God's word. Using Girardian language regarding the choice between two kingdoms, John Desmond recasts the alternatives in O'Connor's fiction thus: "whether to accept the message of Jesus and turn the violence inward against their 'natural' selves for the sake of membership in the kingdom of love (charity) preached by Jesus or to follow the kingdom of violence to its inevitable consequences."[8] Tarwater chooses the kingdom of love.

IMITATING CHRIST BY EMBRACING SUFFERING

In their answer to the problem of violence, Dostoevsky and O'Connor rely on their knowledge of God's kingdom. Although the kingdom of violence rivals God's eternal kingdom, the invitation for citizenship in his kingdom of love has always been open to everyone to choose God as sovereign. Rather than pretending to rule one's own life, potential citizens must renounce their own authority by imitating the King's Son, Jesus Christ. In the Gospels, Jesus says, "Whoever finds his life will lose it and whoever loses his life for my sake will find it" (Matthew 10:39). Girard explains the gospel wisdom with his own aphorism: "Following Christ means giving up mimetic desire."[9] Freedom paradoxically accompanies surrender when the authority is sin-releasing Christ. Imitating Christ is the only way to overcome the satanic mimesis, for only he provides a self-emptying model, thus ceasing the cycle of rivalry that always led to violence.

---

7. O'Connor *The Habit of Being*, 382. O'Connor credits her interpretation to St. Thomas and St. Augustine in another letter (July 25, 1959): "The violent are not natural. St. Thomas's gloss on this verse is that the violent Christ is here talking about represent those ascetics who straining against mere nature. St. Augustine concurs" (*The Habit of Being*, 343).

8. Desmond, "Violence and the Christian Mystery," 130.

9. Girard, *Things Hidden*, 431.

For Dostoevsky and O'Connor, the choice between models arises most clearly when people confront suffering. Ralph Wood associates Dostoevsky's and O'Connor's responses to this problem: "Like Dostoevsky, O'Connor attempts no intellectual answer to the problem of evil. . . . Instead, she is concerned about our proper response to inexplicable horrors suffered by the world's wretches."[10] While neither author may sufficiently explain the coexistence of a just God in an unjust world, they believe purpose and meaning are to be found in suffering. Girard declares:

> However large a part of 'sound and fury signifying nothing' there may be in public and private suffering, in the anguish of mental patients, in the deprivations of the poor and in the rivalries of politics, these things are not lacking in significance, if only because at each moment they are open to the ironic reversal of the judgment against the judge that recalls the implacable functioning of the gospel law in our world.[11]

The temptation to deny meaning in misfortune is powerful, but Girard cautions people against accepting this response. While pain appears meaningless, it can be made to reclaim its significance insofar as the gospel inverts notions of defeat and victory. The sufferers, those who seem most defeated by the world, actually receive the victory. When considered in light of Christ's redemptive suffering, human misery is not meaningless. O'Connor writes, "I believe that everybody, through suffering, takes part in Redemption."[12] Rather than asking why suffering occurs, the question should be how to respond to it.

In addition to Christ, Job is a biblical model commonly associated with suffering. When Job protests his agony, God replies with a series of questions that remind Job of his place in the universe. He asks whether Job can make the sun rise or the tide recede. Essentially, God asks Job, "Who is like God?" After asserting his sovereignty over creation, God demands that Job answer his question: "Will you disannul my judgment? Will you condemn me so that you may be righteous?" (Job 40:8). According to God, in this story, not understanding his ways does not validate rebellion. Finally, Job accepts God as sovereign and humbly confesses, "I spoke of things I did not understand, things too wonderful for me to know" (Job 42:3).

10. Wood, *Christ-Haunted South*, 196.
11. Girard, *Things Hidden*, 446.
12. O'Connor, *Collected Works*, 921.

While Job never receives a rationally satisfying answer from God, he is humbled by the drastic theophany he is given. O'Connor was worried that too many Christians seek to bypass the anguished doubt of Job. "We Catholics," she confesses, "are very much given to the Instant Answer."[13] Unfortunately, fiction, like life, "doesn't have any. It leaves us," O'Connor writes, "like Job, with a renewed sense of mystery."[14] Dostoevsky's Father Zosima understands this mystery, which inspires mimetic acceptance by his hero Alyosha.

For Dostoevsky, Ivan's rational points could only be refuted with a narrative example. Dostoevsky hoped his depiction of Zosima would provide an adequate response to Ivan's argument. In an 1879 letter, Dostoevsky calls the tale "the answer to that whole *negative side*."[15] He planned for Zosima's story to "*compel [nay-sayers] to recognize* that a pure, ideal Christian is not something abstract but is graphically real, possible, obviously present, and that Christianity is the sole refuge for the Russian land from all its woes."[16] "Nay-sayers," as Dostoevsky labels those who concur with Ivan, have a tendency toward abstraction, which Dostoevsky counters with a concrete description of Zosima's Christianity.

Following Ivan's litany of tortured children, Dostoevsky recalls the story of Job in Zosima's hagiography. Frank connects Ivan's protest to Job's:

> No Judeo-Christian reader can help but think of the Book of Job in this connection. . . . Although there is no explicit reference to Job in the notes for these chapters, his name appears three times in other sections; and Father Zosima will narrate the story of Job, stressing its consolatory conclusion in his departing words.[17]

Recounting the story with tears, Zosima exclaims, "And how much that is great, mysterious and unfathomable there is in it!"[18] Zosima's delight in Job's suffering would seem uncaring if it had not succeeded a story of his own grief for his dead brother. By depicting Zosima's response to Job's story, Dostoevsky implies his desire to replicate mimetic response from his readers. Those who hear Zosima's hagiography should be similarly affected by the way in which Zosima read of and emulated Job's submission to God.

13. O'Connor, *Mystery and Manners*, 184.

14. Ibid., 185.

15. Dostoevsky, *The Brothers Karamazov*, 761.

16. Ibid., 760.

17. Frank, *The Mantle of the Prophet*, 429.

18. Dostoevsky, *The Brothers Karamazov*, 270.

Like the layers of imitation found in St. Augustine's *Confessions* in which the saint converts after hearing the testimony of Ponticianus, who converted after reading the story of St. Anthony, who renounced all his worldly possessions after hearing the Gospels read aloud, so does Dostoevsky here create a rousing conversion narrative.

Dostoevsky shows his hero Alyosha initially falling into doubt upon facing suffering but then imitating Christ through the stories that he hears. After the death of his beloved Elder, Alyosha endures a wavering in his faith similar to Job's questioning of God. The decaying of the corpse has caused frenzy among the local congregants, augmented by the ramblings of Father Ferapont who believes that the body's odor is a sign of God's displeasure. The reason that such a ridiculous response compels Alyosha to leave the church is because his love has been "wholly concentrated, perhaps even incorrectly, mainly on just one being . . . on his beloved elder, now deceased."[19] Zosima has been his model but not as a mediator between Alyosha and Christ, rather a substitute for Christ. He begins a descent away from Christ, which is furthered by the instigation of Rakitin who lures him to Grushenka's house with the intention of watching Alyosha "fall . . . from the saints to the sinners."[20]

Alyosha does "fall" in that he allows Grushenka to nuzzle him and crawl into his lap; he sips champagne and he eats sausage, but his real descent occurs in his heart—the doubt he experiences, as he tells Rakitin, "I came here seeking my own ruin." Yet Grushenka's pity changes him.[21] Because of her compassion towards him, he sees her exalted and himself "the lowliest of the accused."[22] When Alyosha returns to the church and hears the story of the miracle at Cana of Galilee read over his Elder's body, he falls before the coffin "as if it were a holy thing" and instead of gnawing grief, he feels joy "shining in his mind and in his heart."[23] By descending first—both his spiritual drop and his literal prostration, Alyosha paradoxically begins to rise. Listening to the story of the first miracle, Alyosha inhabits the story and acknowledges how he is a vessel for new wine. The story becomes a vision of his Elder speaking to him, and he perceives something heavenly

19. Ibid., 339.
20. Ibid., 343.
21. Ibid., 355.
22. Ibid.
23. Ibid., 359.

"descend into his soul."[24] Through his wayward move away from grace, followed by the intentional descent before the coffin, and then his acceptance of the vision from the narrative, Alyosha transforms: "He fell to the earth a weak youth and rose up a fighter, steadfast for the rest of his life."[25] The structural move of Zosima and Alyosha from descent to ascent embodies the epigraph of the novel from the book of John, for each acts as a seed dying to himself to bear fruit. First, Zosima imitates Christ, and then Alyosha follows his Elder. Here, positive mimesis engenders the kingdom of love.

In O'Connor's third unpublished novel—which Bill Sessions has called her most Dostoevskian work—she attempts to write a similar conversion of character in contrast to the violent revolutions that occur in the rest of her fiction.[26] O'Connor explains in a letter, the year before her death, that her current work aimed at accomplishing "larger things," though she does not designate what this entailed.[27] Earlier in the letter, she argues that the writer must make "corruption believable before he can make grace meaningful," a goal she attained in her two novels and short story collections.[28] However, the emphasis changes in her final work to start with the action of grace. The manuscripts for *Why do the Heathen Rage?* focus on Walter Tilman, an inhospitable youth reminiscent of Asbury or Julian, but one who reads saints lives and theology in his spare time. Although Walter surrounds himself with such a library, he has not been reading for edification. The resources have been a matter of pride, not inspiration towards humility.

The catalyst for Walter's conversion is a pen pal Oona Gibbs, a New York social activist whose well-meaning service of the poor stems from misguided tenderness, not unlike the fumbling "good" deeds of Rayber or Shepherd. Gibbs is a founding member of Friendship, Inc., which aims to suffer alongside the oppressed, a somewhat erroneous effort to enact Zosima's advice to be responsible for all. When Walter imagines her commune, "the whole pack of lean, hungry-eyed young people, moving from place to place on the scent of injustice," "their naivete and self-righteousness, their

---

24. Ibid., 363.

25. Dostoevsky, *The Brothers Karamazov*, 363.

26. In conversation with Bill Sessions at the Flannery O'Connor Conference in Rome, 2009. Sessions pointed me toward the unpublished manuscripts, advising me that it showed the most Dostoevskian influence.

27. O'Connor, *Collected Works*, 1184; letter to Sister Mariella Gable (May 4, 1963).

28. Ibid., 1182.

yearning for martyrdom" enrages him.[29] Walter interprets this group, and especially Gibbs, as those who like Dostoevsky's Inquisitor, abrogate the place of God in fixing the state of the world. His animosity towards Gibbs's efforts first persuades him towards accepting the existence of God.

Unlike O'Connor's previous depictions of grace as violent, in this narrative, she renders Walter's awakening in a similar fashion to Alyosha's vision in the church. Uninvited, God ascends Walter's soul towards knowledge of Him: "Without startling him, the answer came, fully formed, fully rational, not wholly [sic] unexpected . . . he believed in God."[30] He is moved by the recollection of the gospel as it has been enacted throughout church history: he lists out the models of Bonaventure, Aquinas, Abelard, and even Luther. Fearful of what this new belief would mean for his life, Walter avoids his former books. However, one day, he picks up the *Letters of St. Jerome*, and reads an admonishment from Jerome to a soldier Heliodorus who had abandoned the contemplative life. Although the language in the letter is implicitly violent because of the military metaphor, the message is ultimately to "seek the sun," or analogously, the Son.[31] After reading such a letter, Walter imitates Jerome and drafts a rebuke to Oona, which he desires to conclude with a quotation on love.

Because these episodes occur at the start of O'Connor's novel-in-progress, Walter's transformation is incomplete. The commencement of good intentions is thwarted by his former self. While Walter may now believe in God's existence, he has yet to lay down his autonomy in preference of God's rule. One may only guess at O'Connor's plans for this character, though perhaps she knew little more of his direction than we do, years later. Walter is unfinished, but the initiation of his trajectory indicates a change in O'Connor's methods. He offers an example of O'Connor's ability to portray positive mimesis, to show how a character might imbibe the gospel and be propelled towards imitation, even if such a new way of living would take time to develop. The unpublished manuscript prefigures a drama between two alternative ways of seeing God's world and sides against those trying to correct Christ's work.

29. O'Connor, "Why do the Heathen Rage?," folder 222, p. 27.

30. Ibid., 226a,19.

31. Letter to Heliodorus, quoted in O'Connor, *Collected Works*, 800

IMITATING CHRIST THROUGH THE LOVE
OF SUFFERING CHILDREN

When Oona Gibbs explains her desire to aid the suffering, she uses language reminiscent of the lady of little faith from *The Brothers Karamazov*. She resides in New York but she dreams of moving to the South and living with a "Negro" family because, as she writes, her "heart bleeds for the poor black people of the South."[32] Oona loves in dreams and at a distance. Like Ivan, who theoretically loves the abused children, she desires immediate gratification for her good efforts. Unlike Ivan, she attempts to act on behalf of the sufferers in her midst, though not in a way that truly helps. Her community huddles together in an apartment as witnesses on behalf of the poor, yet one cannot imagine that the poor receive anything beneficial from their protest.

The example of Alyosha contrasts with the tenderness expressed by the Oonas and Ivans of the world. Alyosha imitates Christ by embracing the children around him. Girard perceives, "The same reasons that distance the rebel from Christ impel those open to love toward him. Alyosha well knows that the pain he experiences at the thought of the suffering children comes from Christ himself."[33] Like Christ, who gathers the children to him in the New Testament, Alyosha draws the young mourners together at the funeral of Illyusha. While the death of the child is another warrant for Ivan's rejection of God, Dostoevsky reveals how it can also unite community. Alyosha does not preach about Ilyusha's resurrection, but about the hope that the children's memory of this event will engender goodness in them:

> [W]hen we recall how we buried Illyusha, how we loved him in his last days, and how we have been talking like friends all together, at this stone, the cruelest and most mocking of us—if we do become so—will not dare to laugh inwardly at having been kind and good at this moment! What's more, perhaps, that one memory may keep him from great evil.[34]

At the end of *The Brothers Karamazov*, Alyosha focuses on Ilyusha's memory in the lives of those gathered at his grave. His words recall Zosima's salvific memories of childhood. Perhaps these children will ultimately become like Zosima, who was long ago saved by the memory of a suffering child: "for

32. O'Connor, "Why do the Heathen Rage?," 218a, 6.

33. Girard, *Resurrection*, 135.

34. Dostoevsky, *The Brothers Karamazov*, 734.

all my childhood rises up again before me, and I breathe now as I breathed then, with the breast of a little child of eight."[35]

In her introduction to *A Memoir of Mary Ann*, O'Connor cites Ivan's rejection of God; however, she does so only after listing out the counter-examples by Nathaniel Hawthorne of those who embrace children such as Mary Ann. Hawthorne's daughter Rose founded the order of nuns under whose care Mary Ann was placed until she died. For O'Connor's purposes, she recounts both Hawthorne's biographical experience and fictional representation of meeting "a wretched and rheumy child, so awful-looking that [Hawthorne] could not decide what sex it was."[36] This miserable "it" reaches out to Hawthorne, who faces the choice of whether or not to pick up the child. In the fictional encounter in *Our Old Home*, which O'Connor mentions, Hawthorne describes the protagonist undergoing a "struggle in his mind," and in his autobiographical account, he calls the struggle "my undesirable burden."[37] For Hawthorne, the choice to embrace the child was neither clear nor easy. He struggles between disgust and pity, but he admits, in his notebooks published posthumously by his wife, "I should never have forgiven myself if I had repelled its advances."[38] This encounter with the child forces Hawthorne to choose between embrace and rejection of suffering. Near the end of her essay, O'Connor calls his choice "a small act of Christlikeness."[39] Hawthorne also connects this choice with Christ, for in his fictional account, he describes it as affecting the protagonist's "final salvation."[40] O'Connor and Hawthorne recognize this embrace as an imitation of Christ, and in both accounts, Hawthorne writes that he acted towards the child like a father. Choosing to embrace the suffering child is, by the inspiration of the Holy Spirit, an imitation of both the Son and the Father.

Like Hawthorne who twice recounts his embrace of the suffering child, Dostoevsky records an encounter with a suffering child in two separate accounts, one autobiographical and one fictional. When Dostoevsky visited London in 1863, he was approached by a six-year-old girl who appeared to be a beggar. Touched by her despair, Dostoevsky records the

35. Dostoevsky, *The Brothers Karamazov*, 270.

36. O'Connor, *Collected Works*, 824.

37. Ibid.

38. Ibid., 825.

39. Ibid., 831.

40. Ibid., 825.

encounter autobiographically in his journal, as well as in a fictional version "The Dream of a Ridiculous Man." In contrast to the author Dostoevsky, who gives money to the poor girl, the ridiculous man stamps his foot and shouts at her as though she were a dog. She immediately flees, searching for someone to help her. The ridiculous man, later recalling this incident, asserts that this poor child saved his life: "I was going to shoot myself. . . . And I should of course have shot myself, had it not been for the little girl."[41] The ridiculous man does not help the despairing girl, nor does his salvation appease her pain. Thus may there be something deeply ridiculous about his final affirmation: "The main thing is to love your neighbor as yourself—that is the main thing, and that is everything, for nothing else matters. Once you do that, you will discover how everything can be arranged."[42] The last line of the story is, "And—I found that little girl. . . . And I shall go on! I shall go on!"[43] In embracing the suffering child, the ridiculous man discovers life.

IMITATING CHRIST: LIKE A CHILD OR LIKE AN IDIOT

Instead of assuming the place of arbiter, Dostoevsky and O'Connor both summon their readers, at least implicitly, to follow Christ's imperative in Matthew 18 to become like a child. Against the pride of their characters, Dostoevsky and O'Connor offer the same guidance as Christ does to his disciples: humble yourselves like children. Elaborating on Dostoevsky's attention to children, Romano Guardini writes in his essay on *The Idiot*, "If you know Dostoevsky at all, you know that in his work men that are wise and pious have a special affinity with children."[44] While Guardini refers here to Prince Myshkin, the connection between piety and love for children occurs also in *The Brothers Karamazov*. Guardini notes that for men like Zosima, "children are a religious mystery; in their souls, which are close to God, there remains something of Paradise."[45] As though recalling paradise, Zosima ruminates on his childhood.

In his account of his childhood, Zosima emphasizes not only the suffering he endured at the death of his brother, but also the young boy's

41. Dostoevsky and Magarshack, *The Best Short Stories of Fyodor Dostoevsky*, 268.

42. Ibid., 285.

43. Ibid.

44. Guardini, "Dostoevsky's Idiot, A Symbol of Christ," 365.

45. Ibid.

dying words, which Zosima exalts as the highest instruction for Christian life. After Ivan's description of tortured children and his rant against God's goodness, Alyosha records Zosima's story in which a suffering child affirms God's goodness. Zosima's older brother Markel, originally an atheist, attends church to appease his mother and eventually converts to the faith. On his deathbed, Markel describes his life as "glad and joyful" and a "paradise."[46] Markel's reaction to his approaching death seems irrational; the doctors fear that his disease is affecting his brain. Markel tries to explain his joy in life, confessing his former sins against nature and other people. He advises his loved ones to imitate his humility: "[E]veryone is really responsible to all men for all men and for everything . . . . Though I can't explain it to you, I like to humble myself before them, for I don't know how to love them enough."[47] Markel's words remain with Zosima, and he repeats them as counsel to the monks at his bedside.

In O'Connor's fiction, the innocence of the child is represented by the "idiot." Bishop, the "idiot" son of Rayber, is "a kind of Christ image," in O'Connor's words, "though a better way to think of it is probably a redemptive figure."[48] Because his uncle Mason believes in the boy's indefinable value, he insists on baptizing Bishop despite his mental deficiency. Mason declares, "Precious in the sight of the Lord, even an idiot!"[49] In defiance of the world's logic and Rayber's pride, Mason conducts himself according to an unseen world that transcends mere reason. Such a practice, Rayber says, constitutes "idiocy."[50] When Bishop is both drowned and baptized at the end of the novel, the scene should convict both readers who believe as Mason does and those who agree with Rayber: for the former, the baptism offers a second life despite the loss of the first and for this other readership, the drowning is only horrifying if one values Bishop's life. If Bishop is as worthless as Rayber deems him, the drowning is inconsequential. Rowan Williams observes, "[C]ertain sorts of suffering draw out from us the most unchallengeable intuitions we have about the transcendent value of human persons."[51] If it is idiocy to baptize this unthinking person, what do we call his death?

46. Dostoevsky, *The Brothers Karmazov*, 265.

47. Ibid., 268–69.

48. O'Connor, *The Habit of Being*, 191.

49. O'Connor, *Collected Works*, 350.

50. Ibid., 389.

51. Williams, *Language, Faith and Fiction*, 232.

O'Connor's stories are cluttered with a variety of idiots, but it depends on the reader to determine their value. While Bishop is a literal "idiot" who represents a model for adult innocence, O'Connor's character Mrs. Greenleaf is an adult who chooses to appear an idiot in the eyes of the world. Although the story revolves around Mrs. May, O'Connor titles it "Greenleaf," underscoring the significance of this marginal character. Daily Mrs. Greenleaf undertakes what she calls "prayer healing": "Every day she cut all the morbid stories out of the newspaper—the accounts of women who had been raped and criminals who had escaped and children who had been burned and of train wrecks and plane crashes and the divorces of movie stars," then she buries them in the woods and prays over them.[52] Prostrate in the dirt before Christ, Mrs. Greenleaf submits to the God whose ways she cannot fully understand. Unlike Ivan, who uses newspaper clippings of others' suffering to fuel his metaphysical rebellion, Mrs. Greenleaf grieves and prays over the afflicted.[53]

CONCLUSION: READERS' IMITATION

Although Father Zosima and Mrs. Greenleaf and other "good" characters appear markedly different from Ivan Karamazov or Mrs. May, the scandal of Dostoevsky and O'Connor is that there are no "good guys." O'Connor explains that all great fiction must demonstrate "a total experience of human nature," which means a depiction of "original sin," of characters who are lacking and incomplete and potentially evil.[54] For some readers, O'Connor's obsession with illustrating the evil side of human beings makes her a misanthrope. True, if one looks for spiritual poverty in O'Connor's oeuvre, one will not have to seek to find it. However, her focus is *exposing* the dearth of faith as a problem. She does not hate human beings, but she believes that we are all "goods under construction."[55] Yet, readers who prize the easy read, the book with clear bad guys and good guys and a worldly happy ending, will not find this reflection of human nature comforting.

Dostoevsky may have to bear fewer insults from his Christian readers, but there are those who are profoundly uncomfortable with his murder and suicide count, not to mention the proliferation of demons. Such probing

52. O'Connor, *Collected Works*, 505.
53. Srigley, *Dark Faith*.
54. O'Connor, *Mystery and Manners*, 167
55. Ibid.

into darkness may lead readers to consider the author himself demonic. To these potential critics, Girard argues, "The novelist is not the devil but his advocate, *advocatus diaboli*. He preaches the false in order to lead us to what is true."[56] While O'Connor and Dostoevsky write stories that suggest they are on the devil's side, as some have accused them, a closer look reveals that they are merely giving the devil his due. Their ultimate goal is transformation, a transformation that is violent, that demands death.

After all, their stories imitate what they consider to be the most scandalous story of all: the death of God, the crucifixion of Jesus Christ. For Dostoevsky and O'Connor, even the good guys, perhaps especially the so-called good guys, will face death. Thus, their fiction is a stumbling block for the same reason that the gospel does not appear to everyone to be good news. The naysayers against O'Connor's violence should remember that the most contemptible characters catch glimpses of grace: recall Mrs. McIntyre or Ruby Turpin. Even murderers, such as her two novels' protagonists, Hazel Motes or Francis Marion Tarwater, are sent out into the world like reformed Karamazovs to bring visions of light to the world and messages of the terrible speed of God's mercy.

Their stories become vehicles of transformation because of their scandal. Readers should find the violence of Dostoevsky's and O'Connor's fiction discomfiting because, through them, the authors show that violence is the unacknowledged choice of their culture. While readers decry violence, they continue to encourage it by believing in the lie of their own autonomy, not to mention the false claims of scientists, politicians, and so forth that they can save the world. Both of these delusions abrogate the place of God and dismiss him altogether. In contrast to these prevalent deceptions, Dostoevsky and O'Connor argue, through their stories, that violence and horror are impossible to dispel without God. If readers follow Ivan and Rayber, rejecting God because of violence, the evil still remains. Violence does not dissipate with atheism. On the contrary, as Dostoevsky and O'Connor show, when characters cease to imitate the Trinitarian God, they have no justification for the sacredness of the individual, and thus occupy a world with a penchant for violence.

Yet, Dostoevsky and O'Connor hoped their readers would rescind their illusion of autonomous authority and choose a life of imitation. As artists, they intended to imitate Christ; they wanted the stories to be imitative of him as well; and finally, for readers then to imitate the good in their

56. Girard, *Resurrection*, 68.

works. They desire their readers to model Alyosha and Mrs. Greenleaf more than Ivan and Rayber. Near the end of Dostoevsky's life, he was profoundly moved when "a host of people, youths, graybeards and ladies" accosted him after his Pushkin speech and exclaimed, "You're our prophet. We've become better people since we read *The Karamazovs*."[57] Dostoevsky could never have foreseen that such testimonies would continue more than a century after of his death. In the mid-twentieth century, O'Connor became one of those influenced by *The Brothers Karamazov*, and her transformation led to artistic imitation.

So, what now? Will such beneficial imitation continue? In 2013 a debate about whether current fiction still depicts the faith of Dostoevsky and O'Connor, novelist Randy Boyagoda attracts readers' attention with his opening remarks: "I'm sick of Flannery O'Connor."[58] He continues his intentional apostasy with a line-up of writers that he is sick of hearing about, concluding with Dostoevsky. Boyagoda clarifies his statement by saying that he desires current writers who share the convictions of O'Connor and Dostoevsky. Instead of facing the scandal that could cause transformation, readers choose the safe and comfortable, entertaining stories that allow them to continue living as autonomous selves. While I would be happy to live in a world where Dostoevsky and O'Connor make the best seller list, even more so, I look forward to the next writer who takes up the mantle, the one who reads *The Brothers Karamazov* and *The Violent Bear It Away*, is transformed, and then, becomes *imitatio* Dostoevsky and O'Connor.

---

57. Contino, "Incarnational Realism," 131.

58. Boyagoda, "Faith in Fiction."

BIBLIOGRAPHY

Alberg, Jeremiah L. *Beneath the Veil of the Strange Verses: Reading Scandalous Texts.* Lansing, MI: Michigan State University Press, 2013.

Alighieri, Dante. *The Divine Comedy: Volume 1: Inferno.* Translated by Mark Musa. London: Penguin, 2002.

———. *The Divine Comedy: Volume 2: Purgatory.* Translated by Mark Musa. London: Penguin, 1985.

———. *The Divine Comedy: Volume 3: Paradiso.* Translated by Mark Musa. London: Penguin, 1986.

Arnold, Marilyn. "Sentimentalism in the Devil's Territory." *Literature and Belief* 17.2 (1997) 243–58.

Auerbach, Eric. *Mimesis: The Representation of Reality In Western Literature.* Translated by Willard R. Trask. Introduction by Edward Said. Princeton, NJ: Princeton University Press, 2003.

Augustine. *Confessions.* Translated by Henry Chadwick. London: Oxford University Press, 1991.

Back, Charlotte. H. *The Fugitive Legacy: A Critical History.* Baton Rouge, LA: Louisiana State University Press, 2001.

Bakhtin, Mikhail. *Problems of Dostoevsky's Poetics.* Edited and translated by Caryl Emerson. Introduction by Wayne C. Booth. Minneapolis: Minnesota University Press, 1984.

Batchelor, Stephen. *Living With The Devil: A Meditation On Good And Evil.* New York: Penguin Group, 2005.

Bauckman, Richard. "Theodicy From Ivan Karamazov To Moltmann." *Modern Theology* 4 (Oct. 1987) 83–97.

Baudelaire, Charles. *Paris Spleen.* Translated by Louise Varese. New York: New Directions, 1988.

Belknap, Robert. *The Structure of the Brothers Karamazov.* The Hague, Paris: Mouton, 1967.

"Best Sellers." *New York Times,* November 1, 2014. Accessed November 1, 2014. http://www.nytimes.com/best-sellers-books/trade-fiction-paperback/list.html.

Bieber Lake, Christina. *The Incarnational Art of Flannery O'Connor.* Macon, GA: Mercer University Press, 2005.

Blake, William. *The Marriage of Heaven and Hell.* New York: Dover, 1994.

Bleikasten, Andre. "The Heresy of Flannery O'Connor." In *Critical Essays on Flannery O'Connor*, edited by Melvin J. Friedman and Beverly Lyon Clark, 138–58. Boston, MA: G. K. Hall, 1985.

Bloom, Harold. *The American Religion*. New York: Chu Hartley, 2006.

Bloshteyn, Maria. "Dostoevsky And The Literature Of The American South." *The Southern Literary Journal* 37.1 (2004) 1–24.

———. *The Making Of A Counter-Culture Icon: Henry Miller's Dostoevsky*. Toronto: Toronto University Press, 2007.

"Books: Old Favorites." *TIME Magazine*, January 31, 1938. Accessed December 1, 2008. www.time.com/time/magazine/article/0,9171,759092,00.html.

Boyagoda, Randy. "Faith In Fiction." *First Things*, August 2013. Accessed November 1, 2014. http://www.firstthings.com/article/2013/08/faith-in-fiction.

Brinkmeyer, Robert H., Jr. *The Art And Vision Of Flannery O'Connor*. Baton Rouge, LA: Louisiana State University Press, 1993.

Browning, Preston M., Jr. "Flannery O'Connor's Devil Revisited." *Southern Humanities Review* 10 (1976) 325–33.

Bruss, Neal. "The Sons Karamazov: Dostoevsky's Characters As Freudian Transformations." *The Massachusetts Review* 27.1 (Spring, 1986) 40–67.

Buckley, Michael J. *Denying And Disclosing God: The Ambiguous Progress Of Modern Atheism*. New Haven, CT: Yale University Press, 2004.

Campbell, Dennis M. *Authority And The Renewal Of American Theology*. Philadelphia: Pilgrim, 1976.

Camus, Albert. *The Rebel*. Translated by Anthony Bower. New York: Vintage, 1984.

———. *Resistance, Rebellion, and Death*. Translated and introduced by Justin O'Brien. New York: Alfred A. Knopf, 1961.

Carroll, Paul, ed. and trans. *The Satiric Letters Of St. Jerome*. Chicago: Henry Regnery, 1956.

Cash, Jean. *Flannery O'Connor: A Life*. Knoxville, TN: University of Tennessee Press, 2002.

Cassedy, Steven. *Dostoevsky's Religion*. Stanford, CA: Stanford University Press, 2005.

Chambers, Whittaker. *Witness*. Washington, DC: Regnery, 1980.

Chesterton, G. K. *Orthodoxy*. Sioux Falls, SD: NuVision, 2007.

Ciuba, Gary M. *Desire, Violence, & Divinity In Modern Southern Fiction*. Baton Rouge, LA: Louisiana State University Press, 2007.

———. "'Like A Boulder Blocking Your Path': Scandal And *Skandalon* In Flannery O'Connor." *Flannery O'Connor Bulletin* 26–7 (1998–2000) 1–23.

Contino, Paul. "'Descend That You May Ascend': Augustine, Dostoevsky, and the Confessions of Ivan Karmazov." In *Augustine and Literature*, edited by Robert Peter Kennedy, Kim Paffenroth, and John Doody, 179–204. Lanham, MD: Lexington, 2006.

———. "Fyodor Dostoevsky." In *The Encyclopedia Of Christian Literature*, edited by George Kurian and James Smith III, 296–97. Lanham, MD: Scarecrow, 2010.

———. "Incarnational Realism and the Case for Casuistry: Dmitri Karamazov's Escape." In *The Brothers Karamazov: Art, Creativity, and Spirituality*, edited by Pedrag Cicovacki and Maria Granik, 131–58.

Copleston, Frederick. *A History of Philosophy: Russian Philosophy*. London: Continuum, 2003.

Cowdell, Scott. *René Girard and Secular Modernity*. Notre Dame, IN: University of Notre Dame Press, 2013.

Cowles, Gregory. "Inside the List." *New York Times*, October 8, 2009. Accessed November 1, 2014. http://www.nytimes.com/2009/10/18/books/review/InsideList-t.html.

Delbanco, Andrew. *The Death of Satan: How Americans Have Lost the Sense of Evil*. New York: Farrar, Straus, and Giroux, 1995.

de Lubac, Henri. *Catholicism: Christ and The Common Destiny of Man*. Translated by Lancelot C. Sheppard and Sister Elizabeth Englund, OCD. San Francisco, CA: Ignatius, 1988.

———. *The Drama of Atheist Humanism*. Translated by Edith M. Riley, Anne Englund Nash, and Mark Sebanc. San Francisco, CA: Ignatius, 1983.

———. *The Mystery of the Supernatural*. Translated by Rosemary Sheed. Introduction by David L. Schindler. New York: Crossroad, 1998.

de Rougemont, Denis. *The Devil's Share*. Translated by Haakon Chevalier. New York: Pantheon, 1944.

Desmond, John. "Violence And The Christian Mystery: A Way To Read Flannery O'Connor." *Literature and Belief* 17.1–2 (1997) 129–47.

Dickie, Jane R., Amy K. Eshleman, Dawn M. Merasco, Amy Shepard, Michael Vanderwilt, and Melissa Johnson. "Parent-Child Relationships And Children's Images Of God." *Journal for the Scientific Study of Religion* 36.1 (March 1997) 25–43.

di Renzo, Anthony. *American Gargoyles: Flannery O'Connor and the Medieval Grotesque*. Carbondale, IL: Southern Illinois University Press, 1993.

Dostoevsky, Fyodor. *The Best Short Stories of Fyodor Dostoevsky*. Translated and introduced by David Magarshack. New York: Random House, 2001.

———. *Brat'ia Karamazovy*. Krasnoyarsk, Russia: ACT, 2007.

———. *The Brothers Karamazov*. Edited by Ralph E. Matlaw. Translated by Constance Black Garnett. New York: W. W. Norton & Company, 1976.

———. *The Brothers Karamazov*. Translated by Richard Pevear and Larissa Volokhonsky. New York: Farrar, Straus, & Giroux, 2002.

———. *The Diary of a Writer*. Translated by Boris Brasol. New York: G. Braziller, 1954.

———. *Memoirs, Letters, and Autobiographical Works*. Translated by Ethel Colburn Mayne, John Middleton Murry, and S. S. Koteliansky. New York: E-artnow, 2015.

———. *Notes From the Underground*. Translated by Richard Pevear and Larissa Volokhonsky. New York: Vintage, 1993.

———. *Pis'ma (Letters)*. Edited by A. S. Dolinin. Vol II–IV. Translated by Ralph E. Matlaw. Moscow: 1930, 1934, 1959 (no publisher).

Dostoevskaia, Anna Grigorevna. *Dostoevsky: Reminiscences*. Translated and edited by Beatrice Stillman, with an introduction by Helen Muchnic. London: Wildwood House, 1976.

Douthat, Ross. *Bad Religion: How We Became A Nation of Heretics*. New York: Simon & Schuster, 2012.

Dowbiggin, Ian. *The Sterilization Movement and Global Fertility in the Twentieth Century*. Oxford: Oxford University Press, 2008.

Driggers, Stephen G., Robert J. Dunn, and Sarah E. Gordon. *The Manuscripts of Flannery O'Connor at Georgia College*. Athens, GA: Georgia University Press, 1989.

Edelman, Diana. "Proving Yahweh Killed His Wife (Zechariah 5:5–11)." *Biblical Interpretation* 11 (2003) 335–44.

Edmonson III, Henry T. *Return to Good & Evil: Flannery O'Connor's Response To Nihilism*. New York: Lexington, 2002.

Eggenschwiler, David. *The Christian Humanism of Flannery O'Connor*. Detroit: Wayne State University Press, 1972.

Fitzgerald, F. Scott. *The Great Gatsby*. Rockville, MD: Wildside, 1925.

Frank, Joseph. *Dostoevsky: The Mantle of the Prophet, 1871–1881*. Princeton, NJ: Princeton University Press, 2003.

———. *Dostoevsky: The Seeds of Revolt, 1821–1849*. Princeton, NJ: Princeton University Press, 1979.

———. *Dostoevsky: The Stir of Liberation, 1860–1865*. Princeton, NJ: Princeton University Press, 1986.

———. *Dostoevsky: A Writer in His Time*. Princeton, NJ: Princeton University Press, 2010.

Franklin, Simon. "Nostalgia For Hell: Russian Literary Demonism And Orthodox Tradition." In *Russian Literature and its Demons*, edited by Pamela Davidson, 31–58. Oxford: Berghahn, 2000.

Freud, Sigmund. "Dostoevsky And Parricide." In *Dostoevsky: A Collection of Critical Essays*, edited by René Wellek, 98–111. New York: Prentice Hall, 1962.

Galsworthy, John. *Letters From John Galsworthy, 1900–1932*. Edited by Edward Garnett. New York: Scribner's, 1934.

Garnett, Edward, ed. *Letters From John Galsworthy 1900–1932*. London: Jonathan Cape, 1934.

Gentry, Marshall Bruce. *Flannery O'Connor's Religion of the Grotesque*. Jackson, MI: University of Mississippi Press, 1986.

Giannone, Richard. "Dark Night, Dark Faith: Hazel Motes, The Misfit, And Francis Marion Tarwater." In *Dark Faith: New Essays on* The Violent Bear It Away, edited by Susan Srigley, 11–34. Notre Dame, IN: University of Notre Dame Press, 2012.

Gibson, A. Boyce. *The Religion of Dostoevsky*. Philadelphia, PA: Westminster, 1973.

Gilkey, Langdon. *Society And The Sacred: Toward A Theology Of Culture In Decline*. New York: Crossroad, 1981.

Girard, René. *Deceit, Desire, and the Novel*. Baltimore: Johns Hopkins University Press, 1976.

———."Dostoevsky's Demons." *The Weekly Standard* 7.35 (May 20, 2002) 31–4. Accessed October 11, 2014.

———. *I See Satan Fall Like Lightning*. Translated with a foreword by James G. Williams. Maryknoll, NY: Orbis, 2008.

———. *Resurrection from the Underground: Feodor Dostoevsky*. Edited by James G. Williams. New York: Herder & Herder, 1997.

———. *Things Hidden Since the Foundation of the World*. Translated by Stephen Bann and Michael Metteer. Stanford, CA: Stanford University Press, 1987.

———. *To Double Business Bound: Essays on Literature, Mimesis and Anthropology*. Baltimore: Johns Hopkins University Press, 1978.

———. *Violence and the Sacred*. Translated by Patrick Gregory. Baltimore: Johns Hopkins University Press, 1972.

"The 'God Is Dead' Movement." *TIME*, October 22, 1965. Accessed April 1, 2009. www.time.com/time/magazine/article/0,9171,941410,00.html.

Gooch, Brad. *Flannery: A Life of Flannery O'Connor*. New York: Little, Brown, 2009.

Gordon, David J. *Literary Atheism*. New York: Peter Lang, 2002.

Gretlund, Jan Nordby, and Karl Heinz Westarp, eds. *Flannery O'Connor's Radical Reality*. Columbia, SC: University of South Carolina Press, 2006.

Guardini, Romano. "Dostoevsky's Idiot, A Symbol of Christ." Translated by Francis X. Quinn. *Cross Currents* 6.4 (Fall 1956) 359–82.

———. "The Legend of The Grand Inquisitor." Translated by Sally S. Cunneen. *Cross Currents* 3.1 (Fall 1952) 58–86.

Harpham, Geoffrey Galt. *On The Grotesque*. Princeton, NJ: Princeton University Press, 1982.

Hauerwas, Stanley. *Dispatches from The Front: Theological Engagements With The Secular*. Durham, NC: Duke University Press, 1994.

———. *Naming the Silences: God, Medicine, And The Problem Of Suffering*. Grand Rapids: Eerdmans, 1990.

Hawkes, John. "Flannery O'Connor's Devil." *The Sewanee Review* 70.3 (Summer 1962) 395–407.

Hendin, Josephine. *The World of Flannery O'Connor*. Bloomington, IN: Indiana University Press, 1970.

The Holy Bible. New International Version. Online: Biblica, 2011.

James, William. *The Varieties of Religious Experience: A Study In Human Nature*. Introduction by Reinhold Niebuhr. New York: Crowell-Collier AS39, 1961.

Janzen, J. Gerald. *Job: A Bible Commentary for Teaching And Preaching*. Atlanta, GA: John Knox, 1985.

Julian of Norwich. *Revelations of Divine Love*. New York: Penguin, 1999.

Kilcourse, George. *Flannery O'Connor's Religious Imagination: A World with Everything Off Balance*. New York: Paulist, 2001.

Kinney, Arthur F. *Flannery O'Connor's Library: Resources of Being*. Athens, GA: University of Georgia Press, 1985.

Kirillova, Irina. "Dostoevsky's Markings in the Gospel according To St. John." In *Dostoevsky and the Christian Tradition*, edited by George Pattison and Diane Oenning Thompson, 41–50. Cambridge: Cambridge University Press.

Kroeker, P. Travis, and Bruce Ward. *Remembering the End: Dostoevsky as Prophet to Modernity*. Boulder, CO: Westview, 2001.

Kuehl, John. "The Grotesque and the Devil." In *Alternate Worlds: A Study of Postmodern Antirealistic American Fiction*, edited by John Kuehl, 144–57. New York: New York University Press, 1989.

Lawrence, D. H. "Preface to Dostoevsky's *The Grand Inquisitor*." In *Selected Literary Criticism*, edited by Anthony Beal, 233–41. New York: Viking. 1961.

Leatherbarrow, W. J. *A Devil's Vaudeville: The Demonic in Dostoevsky's Major Fiction*. Evanston, IL: Northwestern University Press, 2005.

———. *Dostoevsky: The Brothers Karamazov*. Cambridge: Cambridge University Press, 1992.

Lewis, R. W. B. *The American Adam*. Chicago: Chicago University Press, 1959.

Lewis, C. S. *The Screwtape Letters*. New York: Harper Collins, 2001.

Macarius. *The Fifty Spiritual Homilies and The Great Letter*. Edited and translated with an introduction by George A. Maloney, with a preface by Bishop Kallistos of Diokleia. Mahwah, NJ: Paulist, 1992.

Magee, Rosemary M., ed. *Conversations with Flannery O'Connor*. Jackson, MI: Mississippi University Press, 1987.

Manschreck, Clyde L. "Nihilism in the Twentieth Century: A View from Here." *Church History* 45.1 (1976) 85–96.

Marks, Steven G. *How Russia Shaped the Modern World: From Art to Anti-Semitism, Ballet To Bolshevism*. Princeton, NJ: Princeton University Press, 2003.

Marleau, Jacques D., Nathalie Auclair, and Frederic Millaud. "Comparison of Factors Associate With Parricide In Adults And Adolescents." *Journal of Family Violence* 21 (2006) 321–25.

Martin, Regis. *Unmasking the Devil: Dramas of Sin and Grace in the World of Flannery O'Connor*. Naples, FL: Sapientia, 2005.

May, Rachel. *The Translator in the Text: On Reading Russian Literature in English*. Evanston, IL: Northwestern University Press, 1994.

McCullers, Carson. "The Russian Realists and Southern Literature." In *The Mortgaged Heart: Selected Writings*, 252–58. Boston: Houghton Mifflin, 2005. Originally published July 1941.

McMillan, Norman. "Dostoevskian Vision in Flannery O'Connor's 'Revelation.'" *Flannery O'Connor Bulletin* XVI (1987) 16–22.

Montgomery, Marion. "Notes from the Catacombs: On Dostoevsky as a 'Southern' Writer." In *The Inner Vision: Liberty and Literature*, edited Edward B. McLean, 51–76. Wilmington, DE: ISI, 2006.

More, Thomas. *Utopia*. Edited by Paul Turner. London: Penguin Classics, 2003.

Muggeridge, Malcolm. "Foreword." *The Gospel in Dostoyevsky: Selections from His Work*. Walden, NY: Plough, 2004.

Murav, Harriet. *Holy Foolishness: Dostoevsky's Novels and the Poetics of Cultural Critique*. Stanford, CA: Stanford University Press, 1992.

Nabokov, Vladimir. *Lectures on Russian Literature*. Edited and introduced by Fredson Bowers. San Diego: HBJ, 1981.

Nichols, James Hastings. *History of Christianity 1650–1950: Secularization of the West*. New York: Ronald, 1956.

Niebuhr, H. Richard. *Christ and Culture*. New York: Harper and Row, 1951.

Nietzsche, Friedrich. *The Portable Nietzsche*. Translated and edited by Walter Kaufmann. London: Penguin, 1977.

———. *Selected Letters of Friedrich Nietzsche*. Translated and edited by Christopher Middleton. Indianapolis: Hackett, 1996.

Nikoliukin, A. N. *Vzaimosviazi literature Rossii I SShA; Turgenev, Tolstoi, Dostoevskii I Americka*. [*Interrelations of Russian and American Literatures: Turgenev, Tolstoy, Dostoevsky and America*.] Moscow: Nauka, 1987.

O'Connor, Flannery. *The Habit of Being*. Edited by Sally Fitzgerald. New York: Farrar, Straus and Giroux, 1979.

———. *Mystery and Manners*. New York: Farrar, Straus and Giroux, 1962.

———. *O'Connor: Collected Works*. Edited by Sally Fitzgerald. Ann Arbor, MI: Michigan University Press, 1988.

———. *A Prayer Journal*. Edited by Bill Sessions. New York: Farrar, Straus and Giroux, 2013.

———. *The Presence of Grace and Other Book Reviews by Flannery O'Connor*. Compiled by Leo J. Zuber and edited by Carter W. Martin. Athens, GA: University of Georgia Press, 2008.

———. "Why Do the Heathen Rage?" Georgia College and State University, Special Collection, Flannery O'Connor Papers.

———. *Wise Blood*. New York: Farrar, Straus and Giroux, 2007.

O'Gorman, Farrell. "'A dry and seedless fruit': Flannery O'Connor's Rejection of the Rhetoric of Eugenics." Paper presented at the International Flannery O'Connor Conference, Rome, Italy, April 21, 2009.

Pachmuss, Temira. "Dostoevsky and America's Southern Women Writers: Parallels and Confluences." In *Poetica Slavica: Studies in Honor of Zbigniew Folejewski*, edited by J. Douglas Clayton and Gunter Schaarschmidt, 115–26. Canada: Ottawa University Press, 1981.

Palaver, Wolfgang. *René Girard's Mimetic Theory*. Lansing, MI: Michigan State University Press, 2013.

Panichas, George. *Dostoevsky's Spiritual Art: The Burden of Vision*. Introduction by Michael Henry. Edison, NJ: Transaction, 2004.

Pattison, George, and Diane Oenning Thompson, eds. *Dostoevsky and the Christian Tradition*. London: Cambridge University Press, 2001.

Prown, Katherine Hemple. *Flannery O'Connor, Fyodor Dostoevsky and the Antimodernist Tradition*. MA thesis, College of William and Mary, 1988.

Randall, John Herman. *The Making of the Modern Mind*. New York: Columbia University Press, 1940.

Ratner-Rosenhagen, Jennifer. *American Nietzsche: A History of an Icon and His Ideas*. Chicago: University of Chicago Press, 2011.

Reuman, Ann E. "Revolting Fictions: Flannery O'Connor's Letter to Her Mother." *Papers on Language and Literature* 29.2 (Spring 1993) 197–214.

Robinson, Marilynne. *Gilead*. New York: Farrar, Straus & Giroux, 2004.

Roger, James Allen. "Darwinism, Scientism, and Nihilism." *Russian Review* 19.1 (1960) 10–23.

Rogers, Jonathan. *The Terrible Speed of Mercy*. Nashville: Thomas Nelson, 2012.

Sandoz, Ellis. "Philosophical Anthropology and Dostoevsky's 'Legend of the Grand Inquisitor.'" *The Review of Politics* 26.3 (1964) 353–77.

Sanger, Margaret. "Editorial on the Eugenic Resolution." March 13, 1925. Accessed August 12, 2014. http://www.nyu.edu/projects/sanger/proposals/neh/MSEM0034.htm.

Sayers, Dorothy. "The Faust Legend and the Idea of the Devil." *Letters to a Diminished Church*. Nashville: W. Publishing Group, 2004.

Simmons, Ernest J. *Introduction to Russian Realism*. Bloomington, IN: Indiana University Press, 1967.

Spivey, Ted Ray. *Flannery O'Connor: The Woman, the Thinker, the Visionary*. Macon, GA: Mercer University Press, 1995.

Srigley, Susan. *Dark Faith: New Essays on O'Connor's* The Violent Bear It Away. Notre Dame, IN: University of Notre Dame Press, 2012.

———. *Flannery O'Connor's Sacramental Art*. Notre Dame, IN: University of Notre Dame Press, 2005.

———. "The Violence of Love: Reflections on Self-Sacrifice Through Flannery O'Connor and René Girard." *Religion and Literature* 39.3 (2007) 31–46.

Steiner, George. *Tolstoy or Dostoevsky: An Essay in the Old Criticism*. 2nd ed. New Haven, CT: Yale University Press, 1996.

Stephens, Robert O. *The Family Saga in the South: Generations and Destinies*. Baton Rouge: Louisiana State University Press, 1995.

Sutherland, Stewart R. *Atheism and the Rejection of God: Contemporary Philosophy and* The Brothers Karamazov. Oxford: Basil Blackwell, 1977.

Sykes, John D., Jr. *Flannery O'Connor, Walker Percy, and the Aesthetic of Revelation.* Columbia, MO: Missouri University Press, 2007.

Tate, Allen. "Flannery O'Connor—A Tribute." *Esprit VIII* (1964) 48–9.

Taylor, Charles. *Sources of the Self: The Making of the Modern Identity.* Cambridge, MA: Harvard University Press, 1989.

Terras, Victor. "The Art of Fiction as Theme in *The Brothers Karamazov.*" In *Dostoevsky: New Perspective,* edited by Robert Louis Jackson, 193–205. Englewood Cliffs, NJ: Prentice Hall, 1984.

———. *Reading Dostoevsky.* Madison, WI: University of Wisconsin Press, 1998.

Thurneysen, Eduard. *Dostoevsky.* Translated by Keith R. Crim. Richmond, VA: John Knox, 1963.

Tlostanova, Madnia. "The Russian 'Fate' of Southern Letters, or Southern Fiction and 'Soviet' Diction." *South Atlantic Review* 65.4, The Worldwide Face of Southern Literature (Autumn 2000) 28–50.

Tolomeo, Diane. "Flannery O'Connor's 'Revelation' and the Book of Job." *Renascence* 30.2 (1978) 78–90.

Vahanian, Gabriel. *The Death of God: The Culture of Our Post-Christian Era.* New York: George Braziller, 1961.

Weisgerber, Jean. *Faulkner and Dostoevsky: Influence and Confluence.* Athens, OH: Ohio University Press, 1968.

Wigzell, Faith. "The Russian Folk Devil." In *Russian Literature and its Demons,* edited by Pamela Davidson, 59–86. Oxford: Berghahn, 2000.

Wilberforce, William. "Parliamentary Speech." May 12, 1789.

Williams, Rowan. *Dostoevsky: Language, Faith and Fiction.* Waco, TX: Baylor University Press, 2008.

Wolterstorff, Nicolas. *Lament for a Son.* Grand Rapids: Eerdmans 1987.

Wood, Ralph C. "By Grace Alone Through Faith Alone." *Christian Ethics Today* 6.4 (2000). www.christianethicstoday.com.

———.*The Comedy of Redemption: Christian Faith and Comic Vision in Four American Novelists.* Notre Dame, IN: University of Notre Dame Press, 1988.

———. *Flannery O'Connor and the Christ-Haunted South.* Grand Rapids: Eerdmans, 2004.

———. "Flannery O'Connor's Witness to the Gospel of Life." *Modern Age* 47.4 (2005) 321–29.

Wyatt-Brown, Bertram. "Nineteenth-Century Russian Literature and Modern Southern Writers." Proceedings of the 15th International Conference on Literature and Psychoanalysis, St. Petersburg, Russia, edited by Frederic Pereira, in *Instituto Superior de Psicologia Aplicada* (1998) 201–14.

Yaeger, Patricia, and Beth Kowaleski-Wallace, eds. *Refiguring the Father: New Feminist Readings of Patriarchy.* Carbondale, IL: Southern Illinois University Press, 1989.

Zuber, Leo J., ed. *The Presence of Grace and Other Book Reviews by Flannery O'Connor.* Athens, GA: University of Georgia Press, 1983.

INDEX